The Year of the Suffering Servant

Getting more out of Sunday Mass in the Year of Mark

Ciarán O'Callaghan, C.Ss.R.

Contents

Welcome	3	*3rd Sunday of Lent*	58	*16th Sunday Ordinary Time*	102
The Season of Advent	8	*4th Sunday of Lent*	60	*17th Sunday Ordinary Time*	104
1st Sunday of Advent	10	*5th Sunday of Lent*	62	*18th Sunday Ordinary Time*	106
2nd Sunday of Advent	12	*Palm Sunday*	64	*19th Sunday Ordinary Time*	108
3rd Sunday of Advent	14	**Eastertide**	66	*20th Sunday Ordinary Time*	110
4th Sunday of Advent	16	*Easter Sunday*	70	*21st Sunday Ordinary Time*	112
The Season of Christmas	18	*2nd Sunday of Easter*	72	*22nd Sunday Ordinary Time*	114
Christmas Day	21	*3rd Sunday of Easter*	74	*23rd Sunday Ordinary Time*	116
The Solemnity of Mary	25	*4th Sunday of Easter*	76	*24th Sunday Ordinary Time*	118
Feast of the Epiphany	28	*5th Sunday of Easter*	78	*25th Sunday Ordinary Time*	120
Baptism of the Lord	30	*6th Sunday of Easter*	80	*26th Sunday Ordinary Time*	122
Ordinary Time I	32	*Ascension of the Lord*	82	*27th Sunday Ordinary Time*	124
2nd Sunday Ordinary Time	35	*Feast of Pentecost*	84	*28th Sunday Ordinary Time*	126
3rd Sunday Ordinary Time	38	**Ordinary Time II**	86	*29th Sunday Ordinary Time*	128
4th Sunday Ordinary Time	40	*Feast of the Blessed Trinity*	88	*30th Sunday Ordinary Time*	130
5th Sunday Ordinary Time	42	*The Body & Blood of Christ*	90	*31st Sunday Ordinary Time*	132
6th Sunday Ordinary Time	44	*11th Sunday Ordinary Time*	92	*32nd Sunday Ordinary Time*	134
7th Sunday Ordinary Time	47	*Nativity of John the Baptizer*	94	*33rd Sunday Ordinary Time*	136
The Season of Lent	50	*13th Sunday Ordinary Time*	96	*Feast of Christ the King*	138
1st Sunday of Lent	53	*14th Sunday Ordinary Time*	98	*Map of the Holy Land*	140
2nd Sunday of Lent	55	*15th Sunday Ordinary Time*	100		

welcome

Before I start to explain how to use this book, let me offer you a word on what it is about. A lot of people say they get little out of Sunday Mass. They cannot hear the readings, they say, or they don't understand them. If you are one of these people, then this book is for you. The fact that you want to get more out of Sunday Mass is actually a sign of your faith and of your belief that this hour on Sunday is very important. What this book will try to do is encourage you to become a little more active in preparing for Sunday Mass and give you a few tools to help.

What you will need

A Bible: You can either use a complete Bible or, if you have a Sunday missal, you can use that instead. I will give you a few hints for finding your way around the Bible and the missal later.

A copy of this book: Each Sunday, there will be a short reflection on the Gospel. I will try to keep it on a page or two, seldom more.

Time: You won't need a lot but it should be quality time – that is time you can enjoy when you switch off from all the other demands of a busy life. You may find you will get more out of this book if you use our programme twice a week – some time towards the end of the week (say, Friday) to prepare for next Sunday and another time during the week (perhaps Wednesday) to refresh your memory on what the readings you heard the previous Sunday were about.

How to use this book

This book is written with several different kinds of readers in mind.

a) Individual use

First are those people who are looking for help to understand the Sunday Gospels. They haven't done a lot of Bible study since their school days. They may not want to join a Bible study group for all sorts of reasons but they are prepared to invest a bit of private time in preparing for Sunday Mass. My advice is to use the book twice: once during the week before the Sunday (e.g. Friday evening) and the second time a few days later (e.g. Wednesday). Here is a suggested way of spending about fifteen minutes on each occasion.

•   Start by taking a little time to calm your

mind and body, perhaps with the help of some breathing exercises.

- Read the Gospel slowly.
- Read the short explanation of the Gospel in this book.
- Read the Gospel again.
- Spend a few minutes thinking about the Gospel and especially about Jesus.
- You may find yourself moving quietly into prayer.
- Read the Gospel one last time and conclude with the Our Father.

b) Group use

The second group of readers are those who are already members of a Bible study group or who would like to start one. Each person needs a Bible or a Sunday missal and a copy of this book. Since the group will probably only be able to meet once a week for perhaps an hour, this is how the group might go about organising its time.

- Start by taking time to allow the group to calm down and get in the mood to read scripture together.
- Someone should read the text aloud, slowly. It might even be a good idea for members of the group to read a few sentences each before passing on the reading to someone else.
- After the reading, stay quiet for a few moments.

- Read the short explanation of the Gospel in this book.
- Re-read the Gospel.
- Discuss the Gospel together. The group leader might find some of the following questions helpful in getting the discussion going: Is there anything you do not understand in this Gospel? What did you find the strangest or most exciting or most helpful thing in the Gospel?
- Read the Gospel again.
- After this final reading, the group will sit quietly for some time, allowing each person to get in touch with Jesus as he appears in the Gospel. End this time either with spontaneous prayers from the group or with the Our Father.
- If the group has more time, it might be helpful to have a brief review of last Sunday's Gospel. What struck you about it since last week? Was there anything in last Sunday's Mass that helped you to see this Gospel in a new light?

c) Family use

The third group of readers I have in mind are the members of a family. How any family will use it will depend very much on the ages of the children. There are no hard and fast rules but here is one possible way. After the evening meal on Friday read the Gospel for the next Sunday. A parent or one of the children, if he or she is old enough, can explain the Gospel using the information in this book. Read the Gospel again, and encourage the children to say what strikes them about it, or even what they do not understand. End with some prayers based on the Gospel and the Our Father.

After the evening meal on Wednesday or some other evening early in the following week, read the Sunday Gospel again. Let the children share how they see it now. End with a prayer.

Finding your way around

To save space, this little guide does not print the text of each Sunday's Gospel. Instead, it uses a short-hand system to help you find it in your Bible. Here are a few hints for finding your way around the Bible. On most Sundays of this liturgical year, the Gospel readings are taken from the Gospel according to Mark. You will find it in the New Testament section towards the end of your Bible. It may help to keep a bookmark here.

Each Sunday, after the name of the Gospel writer (or evangelist), you will see a set of numbers. The first of these is the chapter. Each book of the Bible is divided into a number of chapters. Each chapter is further divided into a number of verses. A Sunday Gospel usually includes a number of verses. To find it, you start at the first verse mentioned and stop at the last. For example, the Gospel reading for the First Sunday of Advent on page 10 is Mark 13:33-37. That means you first have to locate chapter 13 of

the Gospel of Mark. The reading goes from verses 33-37. Now look at the Third Sunday of Advent on page 14. The Gospel reading is John 1:6-8.19-28. That means you have to locate chapter 1 of the Gospel of John. The reading is from verses 6-8 and then from verses 19-28.

If you are using a Sunday missal, finding the readings will be a great deal easier. All you have to remember is that the Sunday readings are arranged over three years. This year is the second year and, depending on the missal you have, it is called either Year 2 or Year B.

Getting started: Introducing Mark

a) Once every three years

The readings for Mass each Sunday are arranged in a book called a lectionary. It is sometimes solemnly carried in during the opening procession to remind us of how important the readings are and it is left either on the altar or the lectern (the stand from which the readings are done and the homily preached). The reader and the priest or deacon read from this book at Sunday Mass. The readings of the lectionary are arranged over a cycle of three years, so that each year the readings on most Sundays are from the same Gospel. That means the Gospel readings are from Matthew in the first year, Mark in the second, and Luke in the third. These Gospels are called the Synoptic Gospels because they follow the same outline (or synopsis) of the story of Jesus. What about the fourth Gospel, John? Because John is a special type of Gospel and has fewer colourful stories than the other three, it is reserved for use during Advent-Christmas and Lent-Easter.

b) Who was Mark?

We do not know the actual original name of the writer of this Gospel. The traditional name of Mark is attributed to Bishop Papias of Hierapolis (ca. 125–150 AD). In 130 AD he claimed that the name of the evangelist was "John Mark," a companion of Saint Peter, who based the Gospel on the recollections of the apostle. However, Papias based his theory on the authority of a man called John the Presbyter, who was an obscure figure from the early Church. Unfortunately, we do not have any texts from Papias (or from John the Presbyter) and most biblical scholars and historians today are sceptical about Papias' theory. In 200 AD Bishop Clement of Alexandria (based on Papias' theory) stated that Mark wrote his Gospel in Rome. This is the traditional theory of the origin of the Gospel.

Contemporary biblical scholars offer a different theory, based on modern ways of understanding and interpreting ancient texts. According to this non-traditional theory, the Gospel was written in the period 68-70 AD, probably in Southern Syria.

This makes Mark's Gospel the first to be written and as such it is the oldest Gospel in the New Testament. Mark's sources were varied and not based on the testimony of Peter. These sources probably included a passion narrative, collections of miracles stories, some apocalyptic traditions (special material about the end of time), along with some teaching sayings of Jesus. It is believed that Mark's community was non-Jewish (Gentile) and was suffering persecution because of its faith in Jesus. Many in the community were giving up their Christian faith and so the community was crumbling at its edges. As a consequence of this traumatic experience, Mark has a somewhat pessimistic view of discipleship, which is evident throughout the Gospel.

c) The plan of Mark's Gospel

Mark was the first to undertake the writing of a Gospel which set out the miracles and teachings of Jesus against the backdrop of his life story. The basic narrative structure followed by Mark is one that was followed later by Matthew (85 AD) and by Luke (90 AD). Mark's plan of the Gospel is as follows:

- The Prologue (Mark 1:1 13)
- The Proclamation of the Kingdom in Galilee (1:14 – 8:30)
- The Journey to Jerusalem (8:31–10:52)
- The Jerusalem Ministry (11:1–13:37)
- The Passion, Death and Resurrection of Jesus (14:1–16:20)

Each of these sections of the Gospel has its own function and, as you read your way through them in the course of Year B, I will show you how they work. But note one thing immediately. Mark has no account of the birth of Jesus. Nor has he any resurrection appearances of Jesus. Mark 16:9-20 does contain some appearances of the Risen Christ but, as we will see later, they have been added to Mark's Gospel by another later hand. This means that during the Christmas and Easter Seasons of Year B, the liturgy must draw on the Gospel traditions of the other evangelists.

d) Mark's persistent question: "Who is he?"

The Gospel is dominated by the question of Jesus' identity. From the outset Mark proclaims Jesus' identity: he is "Jesus the Messiah the Son of God" (Mark 1:1). Twice God the Father identifies Jesus as his own Beloved Son (Mark 1:11; 9:7). As we read through the Gospel we find people struggling with his identity (Mark 2:7; 4:41; 6:2-3; 8:27; 11:28). Yet evil spirits seem to be able to identify him easily (Mark 1:24.34; 3:11; 5:7-8). Peter seems to identify Jesus correctly as the Messiah (Mark 8:29). However, Peter is thinking in terms of a powerful and glorious Messiah, while Jesus is talking about God's Suffering Servant (Mark 8:31; 9:31; 10:33-34.45). Jesus' identity dominates his religious and political trials. At his religious trial the High Priest asks him, "Are you the Messiah, the Son of the Blessed One?" (Mark 14:61). When Jesus says "yes," he is condemned to death.

At his political trial, Pontius Pilate also questions him about his identity – "Are you the King of the Jews?" (Mark 15:2). There is only one person in the Gospel who correctly identifies Jesus and he is neither a believer nor Jewish. He is the unnamed centurion at Calvary who, when seeing the manner in which Jesus dies, confesses, "Truly this man was God's Son!" (Mark 15:39). Mark has written this Gospel for you and tells you of Jesus so that when you ask the question "Who is he?" you will answer, "He is Jesus, the Messiah, God's Son and Suffering Servant!"

Marana' tha
Come, O Lord

The Season of Advent

The word Advent is derived from the Latin *adventus* which means "coming" and refers to the four-week period of preparation for Christmas. *Adventus* is in turn a Latin translation of the Greek word *parousía*, which refers to the future coming or return of Jesus. During the Season of Advent we contemplate two different comings of Jesus into our world. The first of these refers to his birth as our Saviour over 2000 years ago in Bethlehem. The second refers to his future return in glory as Judge at the end of time. In the early Church, Advent was a period in which new converts prepared for baptism. They did this through prayer, fasting and study. In this way Advent was somewhat like Lent. In the Western Churches the Season of Advent begins on the First Sunday of Advent which marks the beginning of the new Liturgical Year.

As with Lent, the liturgical colour for Advent is purple. The only exception is on the Third Sunday of Advent, which is known as *Gaudete* Sunday. The Latin word *gaudete* means "rejoice!" and since the Mass begins with the words of Saint Paul – "Rejoice (*gaudete*) in the Lord always; again I will say, rejoice" (Philippians 4:4) – this Sunday came to be known as *Gaudete* Sunday. On this Sunday the liturgical colour is rose, which symbolizes the anticipated joy of Christmas breaking into the more penitential Advent Season. The theme of the readings during Advent is the preparation for Jesus' second

coming at the end of time, while remembering his birth in Bethlehem. The First Sunday of Advent reminds us that we do not know the exact time of Jesus' return and so should always be prepared. On the Second Sunday of Advent we are introduced to John the Baptizer who prepared people for Jesus' coming by preaching repentance. On *Gaudete* Sunday John clarifies that he is not the Messiah but the one who prepares his way. Finally, on the Fourth Sunday of Advent, we read Luke's account of the annunciation to Mary and her obedient response to God's call.

There are many things in life to keep our attention fixed on the here and now – the collapse of the economy, the banking crisis, the scandals in the Church, our efforts at trying to make ends meet, along with all the other day-to-day cares of living and of being concerned for others. When the huge tsunami devastated north-eastern Japan in April 2011, the Japanese national soccer team came up with a slogan to encourage their suffering people. It read: "With hope we can cope." The Season of Advent calls for our hope-filled attention. It reminds us that, as daunting as our day-to-day worries are, we ultimately place our hope in the ever-loving and compassionate God. That is why with all Christians down through the ages we can cry out yet again in the Aramaic language of Jesus: *"Marana' tha,* Come, O Lord!"

First Sunday of Advent

27 November 2011

Preparing for Sunday
Read the Gospel: Mark 13:33-37

The explanation

Our first encounter with the Gospel of Mark in Year B is not an easy one. The Gospel reading for the First Sunday of Advent comes from one of the most difficult chapters in the book – Mark 13. We meet Jesus in Jerusalem within 72 hours of his death. If you have ever been to Jerusalem, then you will have seen the spectacular view of the city from the slopes of the Mount of Olives. From there you get a panoramic view of the Old City dominated by the golden-roofed Dome of the Rock dating from 691 AD. In Jesus' day the view was dominated by the Temple and its complex of buildings.

Jesus is seated on the Mount of Olives with his disciples who are enjoying the view. As they look at the city, Jesus offers a long and difficult speech which runs the length of the entire chapter (Mark 13:1-37). The text is largely a farewell speech in which Jesus offers his final words to his disciples and encourages them regarding the crises they are going to face in the future. Similar speeches are found throughout the Bible: Genesis 47-50 (Jacob), Deuteronomy 31-34 (Moses), Joshua 23-24 (Joshua), John 13-17 (Jesus) and Acts 20:17-35 (Paul).

What crises might Jesus be referring to? The situation that fits best is the crisis that faced Jerusalem in the time of the First Jewish War (66–73 AD). This was a rebellion of the Jewish people against the emperor that was crushed ruthlessly by the Romans. During the war the Romans utterly destroyed Jerusalem (70 AD). The unrest of the period would have offered a number of challenges to the Christian community. According to the historian Eusebius (263–339 AD), many Christians did in fact flee the city. Many others remained behind and for them, as well as for Christians living among Jewish communities outside Judaea, life must have been quite tense. In such a setting it is quite likely that some might have understood the crisis as a sign of the end of time.

Jesus' disciples live in the time between the destruction of Jerusalem and the end of time. They do not know, and they will never know in advance, when the end of time will come. So Jesus' message to them is to keep alert for they can easily fall prey to false voices and false signs.

The Year of the Suffering Servant

Jesus gives an example. A wealthy man with servants goes on a journey. Before he leaves, he specifies the servants' responsibilities and expects them to be fulfilled. In particular, the servant who is the doorkeeper must be the most alert of all. The references to the four watches of the night (evening, midnight, cock-crow and dawn) may form a link with the story of Jesus' betrayal, trial and crucifixion. The Last Supper will take place at evening (Mark 14:17). His struggle in Gethsemane, arrest and Jewish trial will take place in the middle of the night (Mark 14:32-65). At cock-crow Peter will deny him (Mark 14:72), and he will be sent at dawn for trial before Pilate (Mark 15:1). These will be moments when discipleship will be sorely tested and fail. Nonetheless, Jesus alerts his disciples to be faithful to their calling as his chosen ones.

As long as people have lived on the earth, they have attempted to predict the end of time. All of the predicted dates came and went and still time continues! The movie *2012* (released in 2009) was based on what is known as the "2012 phenomenon." This is a pseudo-scientific theory that predicts that the world will end on 21st December 2012. We will see! Today's liturgy is not about end-of-time-prediction. Rather, it reminds us that, between now and the end of time (whenever that is), living as authentic disciples of Jesus, God's Suffering Servant, is of far more value than useless speculation about the end of time.

Coming back for another look

Read the Gospel passage again later in the week and think about the following:

•   We Christians do not fret about the end of time, especially when predictions are based on pseudo-science and pseudo-religion. Rather we are watchful about our fidelity to Jesus' call.

•   Being a faithful disciple does not simply happen. It requires care, attention, prayer, penance

Second Sunday of Advent

4 December 2011

FOLLOW THE WAY OF THE LORD

Preparing for Sunday
Read the Gospel: Mark 1:1-8

The explanation

From the very beginning Mark states clearly what his book is about – "the good news of Jesus Christ, the Son of God" (Mark 1:1). The opening verse of the Gospel served originally as a title for the entire book. We normally put a book's title on its spine or cover. At the time Mark wrote the Gospel, books had two forms – the scroll and the codex. The codex was similar to our modern books in that the leaves or pages were sewn together and bound within a cover. Several short books might be gathered into a single codex. In such cases, it would be important to distinguish the various books by putting the title at the head of each one. The opening verse would probably have served as the title. This is a common technique found in the Old Testament and Mark uses it also.

The Gospel proper begins by quoting the Old Testament (Mark 1:2-3). The quotation is a composite of texts from two prophets. The first part comes from the prophet Malachi (500–450 BC) – "See, I am sending my messenger to prepare the way before me, and the Lord whom you seek will suddenly come to his temple" (Malachi 3:1). The second part comes from the prophet Isaiah (540 BC) – "A voice cries out: 'In the wilderness prepare the way of the Lord, make straight in the desert a highway for our God'" (Isaiah 40:3). The prophet Malachi believed that the prophet Elijah would come to prepare the way for Israel's Messiah. In Jewish tradition Elijah was taken up into heaven in a fiery chariot (2 Kings 2:11), and would come again to announce the arrival of the Messiah.

We simply don't know why Mark should have mistaken these verses as a single reference to the Old Testament. He may have been quoting from memory and got the verses confused – a good illustration of the case that there are errors of fact in the Bible. Or since in the Old Testament the book of Isaiah stands at the beginning of the prophetic books and the book of Malachi at the end, Mark means to invoke the whole prophetic witness "from A to Z" in support of the expectation of Jesus, Israel's Messiah.

John was not a hermit but rather a "desert preacher." In locating himself by a ford of the Jordan near Jericho on the edge of the Judean desert, he chose an excellent place to get a congregation from the passing caravans of pilgrims on the way to and from Jerusalem. John's preaching was essentially about the need for conversion and the forgiveness of sins.

One of the major differences between Jesus and John is the question of life style. John was regarded as an ascetic (Mark 1:6). The common criticism of Jesus was that he was a glutton and a drunkard who kept table fellowship with sinners (Mark 2:16).

It is worth noting that Mark's Gospel opens and closes with a messenger scene. The counterpart to John's proclamation of the future Messiah is the proclamation of Jesus' resurrection by the young man in the tomb (Mark 16:5-7). In both cases, they are distinguished by their clothes (hairy garment and white robe), while both point to a forthcoming encounter with Jesus who baptizes with the Holy Spirit. As you read through the Gospel, I will point out other sub-sections that also open and close on a similar note. This seems to be part of Mark's narrative style.

Coming back for another look

Read the Gospel passage again later in the week and think about the following:

- The word *gospel* means "proclamation" or "good news." Mark does not introduce us simply to another book in the Bible. Rather, he offers us a new message based on the sayings of Jesus and on the stories that circulated about him.

- The Gospel text for today focuses on our preparation for the Lord's coming – particularly in the use of the quotation from Isaiah. Mark's good news is that even in the midst of desolation, all our hope has been fulfilled in Jesus.

- The "way of the Lord" is one that God has built for us with total tenderness and love. The choice to follow along that way to encounter God is ours alone.

Third Sunday of Advent

11 December 2011

Preparing for Sunday

Read the Gospel John 1:6-8:19-28

The explanation

John the Baptizer is one of the great Advent figures and today's liturgy allows us to hear him speak. While Mark is the first evangelist to introduce us to John, he gives us no detail about John's view of Jesus apart from one brief statement (Mark 1:7-8). So it is that the liturgy turns to the Fourth Gospel in order to hear John's testimony about Jesus. The Fourth Gospel was written around 90 AD and its traditions are very different from those in the Synoptic Gospels (Mark, Matthew and Luke). These traditions represent an independent line of development of the teaching of Jesus. The Gospel's author (traditionally known as John the Evangelist) is unknown. The Gospel is attributed to a figure known as the Beloved Disciple. Some scholars identify this figure with Jesus' disciple John, while others regard him as an anonymous figure. Do not confuse John the Evangelist with John the Baptizer!

What does John the Evangelist say about John the Baptizer and his testimony? Today's Gospel falls into two parts: an introduction to John the Baptizer (John 1:6-8) and an account of his testimony (John 1:19-28). In introducing John, the evangelist is clear: John is not Jesus. He is a "witness ... only a witness" who gives testimony to Jesus. Testimony is a word the evangelist likes to use frequently in this Gospel. John's testimony ultimately will bring others to faith in Jesus.

As the Gospel opens, John gives testimony to a group the evangelist calls "the Jews." The term refers to the Jewish religious establishment who are opposed to Jesus and his radical interpretation of Judaism. Their question to John - "who are you?" - is crucial as John's identity must be clarified before the Gospel can go on to deal with Jesus' identity. John's answer is both solemn and clear: "I am not the Messiah (Christ)." Prompted by further questions he answers tersely and denies that he is Elijah or a Moses-like prophet. Unlike the Synoptic Gospels the Fourth Gospel does not present John as a messianic Elijah figure. Rather, he is a witness to Jesus. When asked again, "who are you?", he answers by quoting Isaiah 40:3. Last Sunday we

The Year of the Suffering Servant

saw how Mark took this quotation and applied it to John. Today John applies it to himself. John's is the voice who announces the Christ and gives witness to him.

Now the Pharisees take up the interrogation of John. In Jesus' day they were a group of very devout Jews who observed all the commandments of the Law. Their concern is about John's authority for baptizing. It seems that John was the first Jew we know of who baptized people in order to cleanse them of sin. That's why he earned the moniker "Baptizer." But John remains faithful to his role as witness to Jesus. Instead of talking about baptism, he focuses on Jesus. John states that he is of secondary importance and that Jesus, the one he witnesses to, is of primary importance. In fact, he is not even worthy to stoop and serve Jesus.

It may not have been the answer the Pharisees wanted, but then John did not "do" political correctness. I know of an employee who works in a multinational company in Ireland, whose staff are Irish. The employee referred to the coming "Christmas holidays." Next day he was warned by management about his use of language. He was told that as a multicultural organization the company could not use the language of any one cultural or religious group to describe its activities. I wondered if the same organization banned Jews from referring to Passover or Muslims from talking about the Prophet or even atheists from invoking Richard Dawkins! Political correctness in Ireland has opted to deal with cultural and religious diversity by pretending it does not exist. In doing so it has reduced Ireland to a bleak, boring, flat, monochromatic landscape.

That's why John the Baptizer is such a wonderful presence in Advent. He strides onto our bleak and boring landscape with a pesky political incorrectness and proclaims Jesus to be who he is – God's Chosen One. Listen to John's voice today, and let his daring testimony encourage you to give your witness also.

Coming back for another look

Read the Gospel passage again later in the week and think about the following:

• "Who are you?" It's the question John has been asked by the priests and it is the crucial question. Because who you are is what you do. If you are no one, you will do nothing-things. If you are a follower of and witness to Jesus, you will do Jesus-like things.

• "Who brought you to church on Gaudete Sunday?" By that I mean who is responsible for your being at Mass, Gaudete and every Sunday? Who have been the faith-people in your life? Who marked you for Jesus? Whose values do you live by? Answer and continue on to Bethlehem!

Fourth Sunday of Advent

18 December 2011

Preparing for Sunday
Read the Gospel: Luke 1:26-38

The explanation

The other great figure of Advent is Mary, the mother of Jesus. Mark has no Infancy Narrative in his Gospel. He never refers to Jesus' mother by her name and has only one direct reference (Mark 3:31) and one possible ambiguous and indirect reference (Mark 3:21) to her. Accordingly, the liturgy today turns to Luke's Gospel for the story of the annunciation to Mary. Luke was probably a well educated Gentile with some knowledge of the Jewish scriptures who converted to Christianity. He was not part of the first followers of Jesus but a second generation Christian, who knew Paul and was not an eyewitness to the events reported in the Gospel. His Gospel was probably written outside Palestine. This would explain Luke's inaccurate knowledge of Palestinian geography and of some Jewish customs. The Gospel was written probably around 90 AD.

Luke likes to introduce a new scene with a change of time, place and characters. The scene immediately prior to today's Gospel is the story of the annunciation to Zechariah (Luke 1:5-25) which took place in Jerusalem. Now the scene changes to Nazareth in Galilee. It is six months since Elizabeth became pregnant and the story now involves a young engaged woman called Mary and an angel called Gabriel. In Mary's day Jewish marriages were usually arranged by the young people's parents. The first formal stage of marriage was the betrothal or engagement. While the couple would now be legally married, they lived apart in their parents' homes for a year. Only at the end of that year would the groom take his wife to his own home and the marriage ceremony would then last for a week.

The message the angel Gabriel spoke to Zechariah (Luke 1:13) has already proven to be true, so we can now trust the message he is about to give to Mary. Gabriel greets Mary with, "Greetings, favoured one, the Lord is with you." The Greek word which we translate as "favoured one" means "one blest or favoured by God."

Why is Mary so described? God has chosen her to be the mother of a child who will be God's Son, whom she will call Jesus. Her child will be superior to John, even though John will be born first.

for a sign. Mary asks, "how can this be, since I am a virgin?" The sign that Mary will receive will be the presence of God's Holy Spirit and the child born of her will be conceived by God's power. Jesus, her son, is both "Son of God" and "Messiah (Son of David)." Then Gabriel tells Mary of Elizabeth's six-month-old pregnancy and adds "nothing will be impossible with God." *Gabriël* in Hebrew means "power of God" or "my power is God."

Such is God's power that it can bring life to both the barren and virginal womb. Mary has heard God's word and so the story ends with Mary giving her trusting and obedient consent to that word. This is crucial, for as powerful as God is, God never forces people against their will. Gabriel leaves. His mission has been successful.

Coming back for another look

Read the Gospel passage again later in the week and think about the following:

• Mary's discipleship began when she accepted God's plan. Yet this could only come about because of God's grace being with her and her previous willingness to trust God in the course of her life. Her discipleship is not one of *conversion* but one of *consistency*. The same is true for us when we are called by God to be obedient and to trust when something important happens in our lives.

• Mary is indeed Jesus' mother. She is also his first and best disciple.

Luke's story is yet another example of "birth annunciations" which are found elsewhere in the Bible: Judges 13:1-25 (Samson); 1 Samuel 1:9-20 (Samuel), and Luke 1:5-25 (John the Baptizer). One of the elements in such stories is that the person receiving the message becomes afraid on hearing it, but then is reassured by the angel. In today's story Mary becomes "perplexed" but Gabriel tells her "do not be afraid." Another element in this kind of biblical story is that the person receiving the message asks

The Season of Christmas

It may come as some surprise to learn that for the first three centuries of Christianity the Church did not celebrate Christmas. The major Church festival was Easter-Pentecost. It was only in the fourth century AD that the Church began to celebrate the events connected with Jesus' life and ministry. These feasts began first to be celebrated in Jerusalem and were linked to the key holy places associated with Jesus. It was the Western Church (Rome) that began the celebration of Christmas. Nobody knows the actual date of Jesus' birth. Based on Matthew's account and the references to King Herod the Great, the accepted year of Jesus' birth is 4 BC, according to our modern (Gregorian) calendar. But in which month was he born? It was certainly not in December or in winter, for Luke tells us that the shepherds were out in the fields with their sheep (Luke 2:8), something Palestinian shepherds did not do in winter time.

The date of December 25th has to do with the winter solstice. For the pagan Romans this astronomical phenomenon became an event of religious significance. They turned the solstice into a two-week religious festival (*Saturnalia*) in which they celebrated the birthday of *Sol Invictus* ("The Unconquerable Sun"). As with many other pagan Roman feasts, the early Christians took it over and sanctified it as the festival of the birthday of the Son of God. Originally the feast was called Epiphany, from the Greek word *epipháneia* meaning "manifestation." When the Eastern Church (Constantinople) eventually adopted Epiphany, it was celebrated on January 6th. Our word "Christmas" is derived from the Old English *Christes Mæsse*, which means "Christ's Mass." The first recorded use of *Christes Mæsse* dates from 1038 AD.

The commercial (and decidedly non-Christian) winter festival of Christmas seems to begin earlier and earlier each year. Last year I saw my first Christmas advertisement in September! I suspect this has to do with businesses trying to survive in our recession-devastated economy. However early it might start, commercial Christmas ends with the close of business on Christmas Eve. The Catholic liturgical Season of Christmas (Christmastide) begins on Christmas Eve with Midnight Mass and continues until the Feast of the Baptism of the Lord, which in Ireland falls on January 8th. The liturgical colour for Christmastide is white.

The Season of Christmas contains many feasts, but three are most important. These are the Feast of the Nativity of the Lord, the Feast of the Epiphany of the Lord, and the Feast of the Baptism of the Lord. The Feast of the Nativity celebrates the birth of Jesus, God's Son, and his revelation to the Jewish world. It has three different liturgical celebrations in one day: Midnight Mass, Dawn Mass and Daytime Mass. The Feast of the Epiphany celebrates not just the arrival of the wise men but Jesus' revelation to the Gentile (non-Jewish) world. The Feast of the Baptism of the Lord celebrates Jesus' baptism when he came face to face with his identity and calling and then began his mission.

Christmastide 2011 is a little more complicated in that Christmas Day falls on a Sunday. The Solemnity of the Mother of God is always celebrated on January 1st, which in 2012 also falls on a Sunday. This means the celebration of the Feast of the Holy Family (which is usually celebrated on the Sunday immediately after Christmas) moves to December 30th and the celebration of the Second Sunday of Christmas does not take place. In Ireland the Feast of the Epiphany is celebrated on Friday, January 6th and Christmastide ends on Sunday, January 8th with the Feast of the Baptism of the Lord. If you live in the UK, the Feast of the Epiphany is celebrated on Sunday, January 8th and the Feast of the Baptism of the Lord is kept on Monday, January 9th. So Christmastide is longer by one day in the UK this year. As I said, it's a bit complicated!

Once again, since Mark does not have an Infancy Narrative, the liturgy draws on the other three Gospels for its readings. At Christmas Midnight Mass we read Luke's account of the birth of Jesus and of his revelation to the Bethlehem shepherds. At the Dawn Mass on Christmas Day we continue reading Luke's account of the visit of these shepherds to Jesus. At the Daytime Mass we read the solemn and majestic introduction to the Gospel of John which also deals with the birth of Jesus who is the eternal and pre-existent Word of God. On the Solemnity of the Mother of God we re-read Luke's account of the birth of Jesus but with the added detail of his naming and circumcision. For the Feast of the Epiphany the liturgy turns to Matthew, for he is the only evangelist who tells of the visit of the Magi to Jesus at Bethlehem. Finally, for the Feast of the Baptism of the Lord we return to Mark for his simple but refreshingly direct account of Jesus' baptism.

Christmas Day

25 December 2011

And the Word became flesh and lived among us

Preparing for Midnight Mass
Read the Gospel: Luke 2:1-14

The explanation

Luke was a historian and wanted to link his account of Jesus' birth to world history. Unfortunately, this creates a bit of a difficulty for those of us who want a modern, precise and verifiable historical account. According to Luke, the census took place under Augustus Caesar (44/42 BC–14AD). There is no evidence available to support his claim that such a census ever took place. Herod the Great (74-4 BC) was the Roman client king who ruled Judaea (37–4 BC) at the time of Jesus' birth. He died in 4 BC, the year Jesus was born. Herod's son, Herod Archelaus (4 BC–6 AD), then ruled Judaea for ten years. Eventually Archelaus was removed by the Emperor Tiberius in 6 AD and banished to France. Archelaus' territory was then incorporated into the province of Syria which was ruled by the Roman Governor Quirinius (6–12 AD). It was Quirinius who held the census of Syria (including Judaea) in 6 AD. It seems that Luke has confused the banishment of Herod Archelaus (6 AD) with the death of Herod the Great (4 BC) and dated Quirinius' census (6 AD) to the time of Herod's death (4 BC). Confusing? Furthermore, the Roman system of registration did not oblige people to travel to their place of birth or of origin and only men could legally carry out any registration required. In short, there is nothing in Roman law that would have required Joseph or Mary to travel to Bethlehem in the first place!

So why is this census important to Luke? First, Luke attempts to "square the circle" of Bethlehem and Nazareth. Jesus was born in Bethlehem in Judaea, the city of Israel's future Messiah. But he grew up in Nazareth in Galilee and began his ministry from there. The census story attempts to explain how this might have happened. Second, Luke wants to link Jesus' birth to world history. He does this with reference to Augustus, Herod, and Quirinius. Third, Augustus is credited as have initiated a period of peace (27 BC–180 AD) in the Roman Empire often known as the *Pax Romana* ("Roman Peace"). Luke presents Jesus as the source of the world's authentic peace. Fourth, Luke is writing his Gospel for Gentiles throughout the Roman Empire. He is concerned to show that Christianity is no threat to the empire. His portrait of Joseph and Mary is of a law-abiding couple.

Finally, there is Luke's theology of the upside-down world of God. Luke delights in showing that God thinks and acts in ways very different to those of human beings. Luke's Roman readers might have expected the Messiah to be born in a palace in Rome. Jesus, the Son of God, is to be found in an animals' feeding trough on the edge of a small village in a territory on the margins of the empire!

Luke's account of the actual birth of Jesus is brief. Its significance may well be in the hidden references to the Old Testament. Jesus is placed in a manger or feeding trough. The allusion is to Isaiah 1:3 – "The ox knows its owner, and the donkey its master's crib; but Israel does not know, my people do not understand." The allusion is to the complaint that the people of Israel do not have a close and intimate relationship with God. With the birth of Jesus that situation is corrected.

Jesus is wrapped in a cloth or swaddled. The allusion here is to the Wisdom of (King) Solomon 7:4 – "I was nursed with care in swaddling cloths. For no king has had a different beginning of existence." Jesus is a royal baby, the son of David and the Messiah.

Finally, there is the famous reference to the "inn." The Greek word (*katályma*) used here means an "upper room" and refers to a communal sleeping place where travellers or pilgrims could rest. The allusion is to Jeremiah 14:8 – "O hope of Israel, its saviour in time of trouble, why should you be like a stranger in the land, like a traveller turning aside for the night?" Jesus is no stranger in Bethlehem; he is born in his own place and among his own people. It may be of interest to know that when Jesus comes to celebrate the Passover meal on the night before he dies, Luke tells us that he chooses a *katályma* or "(guest) room" for the meal (Luke 22:11).

The great news of Jesus' birth is given first to shepherds, who in first century AD Judea would have been regarded as non-kosher (ritually unclean) and dishonest. Again Luke's message about the upside-down world of God is clear. Jesus's birth is first witnessed, not by the powerful and the wealthy, but by the poor and marginal. The angels' message to the shepherds is good news for all peoples, for Jews and Gentiles alike. The angels sing of peace. It is not Caesar's *Pax Romana*. Rather it is a divine gift to all peoples whom God favours.

Preparing for the Dawn Mass
Read the Gospel: Luke 2:15-20

The explanation
The Gospel reading for the Dawn Mass continues Luke's account of the birth of Jesus and its proclamation to the shepherds. Now we hear their response. They talk to each other and travel to Bethlehem. They find Mary, Joseph and the baby and report the message of the angels. That message says everything about Jesus: he is Israel's Messiah and the world's Saviour. When the shepherds find the baby in the manger as the angels had said, it confirms the message about the

child's identity for them. Now they proclaim the good news of that message. These lowly, poor, non-kosher Bethlehem shepherds have become messengers of the Gospel.

Finally, Luke adds another detail about Mary. She is someone who reflects deeply on the meaning of all these events.

Preparing for the Day Mass
Read the Gospel: John 1:1-18

The explanation

For the Christmas Day Mass we read the solemn and majestic introduction to the Fourth Gospel. The Synoptic Gospels all begin with traditions about John the Baptizer. In particular, the Gospel of Luke links these Baptizer traditions to stories about the birth of Jesus. The Fourth Gospel starts in a different manner entirely. Its author takes traditions about the Word of God who is from eternity and blends these traditions with others about the Baptizer. The effect is to create a composite portrait of Jesus who is before time and history and yet who is born and ministers *in* time and history. The evangelist has created this introduction primarily as an overture to the theological themes that will be developed later on in the Gospel. For this reason John 1:1-18 is often called the Prologue to the Fourth Gospel.

The Greek concept of *lógos* ("word") dominates the beginning of the Prologue. In using this term, the evangelist draws on Greek philosophy along with Jewish concepts of creation and wisdom. The effect is to use a concept that has a familiar ring for both Greeks and Jews. Yet the author goes beyond the limits of Greek and Jewish thought to proclaim something radically new: God's eternal and creative Word has entered our world and become one like us. In doing so, the Word offers life to all people in the world and is a light that can never be overcome by the world's evil.

At this point you might like to go back and re-read the Gospel for the Third Sunday of Advent (pages 14-15 above). It was then we were introduced to the Baptizer traditions in the Prologue. The author of the Fourth Gospel is clear that John the Baptizer is not the light. Rather, he gives testimony to the light. In this way the evangelist moves the focus away from Jesus the Eternal Word, who existed before time and creation, to Jesus the Incarnate Word who is present in human history. It is not possible to be neutral where the Incarnate Word is concerned. People will have to make a choice for or against Jesus. The evangelist divides people into two groups. There are those who will not accept Jesus. Then there are those who, in accepting him and believing in his name, will become "children of God."

Probably one of the most famous verses in the whole Prologue is John 1:14 – "And the Word became flesh and lived among us." The Greek text reads literally, "And the Word became flesh and pitched tent among us." While we are familiar with the phrase in the prayer of the Angelus, it is this verse which sums up all that we celebrate in Christmastide. The idea of the Word "pitching a tent" among humanity is one which draws on the richness of the Old Testament. During Israel's wandering in the Sinai desert, the tent was the place where God dwelt (Exodus 33:9). Speaking through the prophet Ezekiel, God made a solemn promise to Israel – "My dwelling place shall be with them; and I will be their God and they shall be my people" (Ezekiel 37:27). The Prologue to the Fourth Gospel affirms on this Christmas morning that God's presence among us is visible in Jesus.

The very last verse of the Gospel reading (John 1:18) brings the Prologue to an end and opens up the Fourth Gospel's account of Jesus' life and ministry. It is Jesus who will make God known. The Greek text is much richer than the English translation. It asserts that Jesus and only Jesus will "bring out" or "interpret" God for us. The reason that Jesus can do this is because he is "close to the Father's heart." He is the Son who has an intimate relationship with the Father and as such is the only one who can interpret God for us. This Prologue does not make for easy reading. Luke's story of the shepherds and the angels might seem more emotionally appealing. Yet, John's Prologue asserts the same truth in rich and complex language: Jesus, God's Son, has come among us as one of us in order to reveal God to us. That's what Christmas is all about.

Coming back for another look

Read the three Gospel passages again later in the week and think about the following:

•	On Christmas Day all roads lead to Bethlehem and all are invited to travel them. Mary and Joseph have travelled as law-abiding citizens. The shepherds have travelled because of the message of the angels. Others travel in search of God's word or because of some deep life-experience. Why do you travel to Bethlehem?

•	Luke claimed that, with the birth of Jesus, the rule of Caesar Augustus had been replaced by a new world order under God. It was an astonishing claim to make 2000 years ago. Today we can easily think that the world order is determined by the EU or ECB or IMF or USA. Luke reminds us that it is God's rule that shapes our world and that, in God's Kingdom, pride of place goes to the lowly, the poor and the marginalized. There is even a place for shepherds!

•	Return again to the phrase "and the Word became flesh and pitched tent among us" in the Prologue (John 1:14). It is an amazing assertion. Ours is not some remote and isolated God. In Jesus, God has chosen to become like us. God has chosen to "learn" what weakness, sickness, pain and grief are like along with friendship, joy and love. Above all, God has chosen to experience human death in all its terror. God has done this for love of you. God has done this that you may live forever.

The Solemnity of Mary, the Mother of God

1st January 2012

Preparing for the Solemnity

Read the Gospel Luke 2:16-21

The explanation

Today's feast is always celebrated on January 1st and this year replaces the liturgy for the Second Sunday of Christmas. While the feast has its origins in the Eastern Church, it was celebrated in Rome by the fifth century AD. By the late Middle Ages it was celebrated in the Western Church under the title of the Feast of the Circumcision of Christ. In the period of liturgical reform after the Second Vatican Council, Pope Paul VI replaced the Feast of the Circumcision of Christ with the Solemnity of Mary, the Mother of God.

In 431 AD the Church gave Mary the wonderful title of *Theotókos*. It is a Greek word which means "God-bearer." In the Western Church this title was translated into Latin as *Mater Dei* or "Mother of God." Unfortunately, it is not an exact translation and usually needs a lot of explanation for English speakers. God is eternal and does not have a source. So the title *Theotókos* does not mean that Mary is the mother of God from eternity. She is the mother of Jesus, who is the incarnate Word of God. It is a profound title which says something about Jesus and about Mary in relation to Jesus. Jesus is the Messiah (Christ) and Son of God. Mary is his mother and as such can be venerated as *Theotókos*.

The Gospel for today's feast is essentially that of the Dawn Mass on Christmas Day. It would be helpful if you read again the explanation for that Gospel text (see pages 23-24). However, today's text is longer by one verse (Luke 2:21). This extra verse adds yet another detail to the story of the birth of Jesus: his naming and circumcision. Both these events give the child his identity. He becomes a member of the community of Israel by circumcision, a ritual for male children which was laid down by the Jewish Law (Genesis 17:12 and Leviticus 12:3).

Yet, for Luke, the key ritual is the naming of the child. He is given the name Jesus. This is our English version of the Greek *Iēsoûs*, which in turn is a translation of the Hebrew original *Yēšûă*. The Hebrew name means "YHWH saves" or "YHWH is salvation" and was a very common name in Judaea of the first century AD. For Luke, it is the name that the angel told Mary to give the child (Luke 1:31) and is God's choice of name for him. Jesus, Mary's son, is God's Son, the Messiah of Israel and the Saviour of all humankind.

Coming back for another look

Read the Gospel passage again later in the week and think about the following:

• Today's feast offers a profound understanding of who Mary is in relation to her son, who is God's Son. It might be a good occasion for you to do some thinking about Mary and the place she occupies (or does not occupy) in your own spirituality and Christian faith.

• The ritual of Jesus' circumcision and naming establishes and proclaims his identity. We have our own Catholic rituals (Baptism, First Communion and Confirmation) which establish and proclaim our identity as followers of Jesus. Secularism, loss of faith and the false sense of wealth of the Celtic Tiger years have eroded the meaning of such rituals and turned them into meaningless and superficial social rites of passage characterized by wasteful excess. The memory of Jesus' naming and circumcision is a challenge to all Catholics who take their faith seriously. How do we recover a sense of God's presence in our everyday lives? Where is the Mystery to be found among us? What have we lost by devaluing and desacralizing our rituals? I know that this all sounds pretty heavy! Yet as you think about these questions, let God guide you to reclaim and proclaim more profoundly your identity as a disciple of Jesus.

Rites of Passage

The Epiphany of the Lord

6th January 2012 (Ireland); 8th January 2012 (UK)

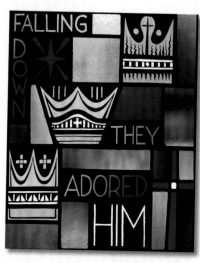

Preparing for the Feast
Read the Gospel: Matthew 2:1-12

The explanation

Today we celebrate Jesus' manifestation (*epipháneia*) to the Gentile world as represented by the Magi. It might come as a surprise to you that Matthew does not refer to "three Magi" but to "some Magi." Nor has Matthew anything to say about "three kings." The word Magi comes from the plural of the Latin word *magus* which in turn is a translation of the Greek word *mágos*, meaning "astronomer," "astrologer," "visionary" or "sorcerer." The term was used mainly of a priestly group of Persian or Babylonian experts who studied the stars in order to understand the will of God.

Since Matthew mentions "three" gifts (gold, frankincense and myrrh), a tradition soon grew up that there were "three" Magi. The early Christians used the Old Testament as a source by which they could better understand Jesus. There are a number of texts in the Old Testament which suggest that Israel's Messiah would be worshipped by kings (Isaiah 60:3; Psalm 68:29 and Psalm 72:10). On

this basis the Magi were soon understood to be kings and by about 500 AD this tradition became so well established that the "three kings" were given their names – Caspar, Melchior and Balthasar. In line with this decidedly non-Gospel tradition, the "three kings" are now claimed to be buried in the Shrine of the Three Kings at Cologne Cathedral. It is a good story – but also a good example of how a religious tradition can wander far from the Gospel. So let's go back to Matthew!

Matthew's Gospel was written some time around 85 AD. The evangelist used Mark's Gospel along with other traditions about Jesus and collections of Jesus' sayings. Biblical scholars today understand that Matthew's community was of Jewish origin and had probably originated in Palestine but eventually settled in Syria. Since Matthew is trying to tell a Jewish community about Jesus, he draws constantly on the Old Testament for texts to show that Jesus is truly Israel's Messiah.

So it is that the Magi ask "where will the infant be born?" They soon discover that the place is Bethlehem, from where Israel's Messiah would come. The Magi also call Jesus the "King of the Jews" even before they see him. Again this is Matthew's way of reminding us that Jesus is from the line of David, which is the lineage of the Messiah.

The Magi make the journey following a star. I'm sure this year someone will come up with yet another theory to explain the star as a natural phenomenon – a conjunction of the planets Jupiter and Saturn or even an alien spaceship or two! For Matthew, the star is something biblical and miraculous. The Old Testament understood that the coming of the Messiah was associated with a "star out of Jacob" (Numbers 24:17). The Magi who come to Bethlehem following a star are pagan Gentiles in search of a Jewish biblical promise.

Unlike the Magi, Herod along with his advisers wishes to do away with such a promise. Notice how Matthew describes Herod's advisers. They are "chief priests" and "scribes." Later on it will be the chief priests and scribes along with the ruler of Judaea (Pontius Pilate) who will do away with Jesus. Herod attempts to enlist the Magi in order to destroy Jesus. He is not interested in worshipping the child, only in destroying him. When the Magi finally arrive at Jesus' house they worship him and give their three gifts. Finally, warned (by God) in a dream, they return home to their land, avoiding Herod and his murderous scheme.

Matthew's story is well known, but it is richer and more profound than the popular telling of it. For Matthew, Jesus' birth is good news for Jews and Gentiles alike. More than that, Jews and Gentiles will have to make up their minds about Jesus – they will have to accept or reject him. The Magi who come to worship Jesus must learn from the Jewish scriptures, while those who have the sacred texts (Herod and his advisers) are not willing to accept Jesus.

Coming back for another look

Read the Gospel passage again later in the week and think about the following:

•   Matthew's story of Jesus' birth prepares us also for his death and resurrection. In both stories a political ruler (Herod or Pilate) wishes to destroy Jesus. The chief priests and scribes conspire against him – but God saves him. Today's feast asks plainly: do you accept Jesus or reject him?

The Baptism of the Lord

8th January 2012 (Ireland); 9th January 2012 (UK)

Preparing for the Feast
Read the Gospel: Mark 1:7-11

The explanation

Today's feast brings Christmastide to an end, taking us beyond the stories of Jesus' infancy and introducing us to him as a young man ready to begin his ministry and mission. The Gospel reading overlaps slightly with that of the Second Sunday of Advent (pages 12-13). You might like to go back and read that text again.

Today we read the first scene in which Jesus appears in Mark's Gospel. It might be helpful to remember that the Gospel stories about the ministry, death and resurrection of Jesus contain three important elements. First, they contain eyewitness material about what Jesus said and did. Second, they are shaped by the early Church's proclamation of Jesus as Messiah, Son of God and Risen Lord. Finally, they are further shaped by the theological perspective of each of the evangelists. The story of the baptism of Jesus is an excellent example of how the different evangelists have used largely the same material with a number of striking

changes to express their own particular theology. Mark tells the story simply and directly (Mark 1:9-11). Matthew has taken up the same story but has added a number of verses, particularly about John's reluctance to baptize Jesus and Jesus' insistence that it should be done as an act of humility (Matthew 3:13 17). Luke describes the descent of the Holy Spirit, offers no description of the baptism itself, and focuses more on Jesus at prayer (Luke 3:21 22). Finally, the writer of the Fourth Gospel makes much of the Baptizer's testimony but offers no account of the actual baptism of Jesus (John 1:19 34).

Today's text begins with the message of John the Baptizer, who is very much like an Old Testament prophet. John points to what God is going to do in the future through "someone more powerful" than he. Even though we have not yet met Jesus in this Gospel, Mark has already introduced him as Messiah, Son of God, Lord and the Mightier One. These last two titles were traditionally used of the God of Israel. Now Mark uses them of Jesus. In order to emphasize how mighty Jesus is, John says that he would not be worthy to untie Jesus' sandals. In Jesus' day not even a slave was compelled to do such a demeaning task. So when John compares himself to Jesus, he says that he is even lower than a slave.

Finally, John says that Jesus will gift people with the Holy Spirit. This was something that Judaism expected the God of Israel to do. So before we even meet him, Mark (through John the Baptizer) has told us that Jesus carries the titles and one of the functions of God.

Having read the infancy stories in the Gospels of Matthew and Luke along with the majestic opening to the Fourth Gospel, your first glimpse of Jesus in the Gospel of Mark may come as something of a surprise. Jesus simply comes from Nazareth and joins a line of people going out to John the Baptizer in the desert. His entrance and baptism are told in a single verse. Mark then goes on to describe the heavens being torn open and God's Spirit descending on Jesus. The Greek text allows us to understand that this was a moment of visionary experience for Jesus. In the Old Testament, such moments of visionary experience were an essential part of the prophetic call or vocation stories – Isaiah 6:1-13 (Isaiah of Jerusalem), Jeremiah 1:4-19 (Jeremiah), and Ezekiel 1:1 – 3:21 (Ezekiel).

Lastly, Mark tells us that a heavenly voice was heard, identifying Jesus as the beloved Son of God on whom divine favour rested. The language has some Old Testament echoes. Isaac was the beloved son of Abraham (Genesis 22:2), while the Suffering Servant was the one in whom God delighted (Isaiah 42:1). Mark presents the baptism scene as one where Jesus comes face to face with his identity as both God's Beloved Son and Chosen One and also where he faces his destiny to proclaim the kingdom of God.

Coming back for another look

Read the Gospel passage again later in the week and think about the following:

- The message of Christmastide can be easily drowned out by the seductive jingle of commercial Christmas. So listen carefully to the message this year.
- The image of "baby" Jesus can easily distract us. Jesus, our Risen Lord, is no baby and he does not call us to infantile discipleship.
- You too were baptized. What does that say about your identity, your destiny and about the way God sees you?

Ordinary Time I

The liturgical period outside the seasons of Advent-Christmas and Lent-Easter is known as "Ordinary Time." This is a translation of the Latin phrase *tempus per annum*, which means "time through the year." Ordinary Time is divided into two periods. Ordinary Time I is the period immediately after the Feast of the Baptism of the Lord up to Ash Wednesday. Ordinary Time II is the period following the Feast of Pentecost up until the First Sunday of Advent.

In 2012 Ordinary Time I runs from Monday, January 9th until Tuesday, February 21st. In the UK, Ordinary Time I begins a day later on Tuesday, January 10th and ends on Tuesday, February 21st. Ordinary Time II runs from Monday, May 28th until Saturday, December 1st. While the Sundays and weeks in Ordinary Time are numbered 1–34, some Sundays are named after the feasts they commemorate. In 2012 these are: Trinity Sunday (June 3rd), the Solemnity of the Most Holy Body and Blood of Christ (June 10th), the Feast of the Nativity of John the Baptizer (June 24th), and the Solemnity of Our Lord Jesus Christ, Universal King (November 25th). The liturgical colour for Ordinary Time is green.

You can now begin to read the Gospel of Mark seriously and systematically on each Sunday in Ordinary Time. This Gospel was seen as a bit of an ugly duckling by the early Christian Church when compared with the other Gospels. It was argued that Mark's Gospel was nothing more than a summary of Saint Peter's thoughts written in too-simple Greek, with poor sentence construction and an unattractive narrative style. So the early Christian Church turned repeatedly to Matthew's Gospel for inspiration and guidance.

As the Church began to grow, it looked to the scriptures for proof-texts for its theology. These were texts that could be used to support its theological positions on many issues. In this regard, Mark's Gospel offered little or nothing. In fact, the Gospel may only have survived because the Church considered it to be a text shaped by Saint Peter's recollections and written in Rome – a viewpoint no longer supported by mainstream biblical scholarship! It is only in the last 200 years that the importance of Mark's Gospel has been re-discovered and it is now given its rightful status and recognition in the New Testament.

This Gospel has been variously described as sombre, stark and even as the scariest of the four Gospels. It is a scary Gospel because it is dominated by the theme of demonic possession. People in Mark's day used the concept of "demonic possession" to describe any force that enslaved them. They recognized that there were forces in life over which they seemed to have no control. These forces took away their freedom of choice, crippled their human growth, separated them from God and others, and even alienated them from their own humanity.

They also believed in a supreme force of evil called Satan. They called all such forces "demons" and were terrified of them. We recognize such forces today and the slavery they create in us and in our world. We talk about "confronting our demons." We might feel a little too sophisticated to talk about Satan, but we know that the force of evil is at large in the world and it is truly destructive. Mark's message for us is clear: only Jesus can free us from Satan and all the other "demons" that enslave us.

This is a stark Gospel because it deals with the theme of failed discipleship. For Mark, it is fear that utterly destroys discipleship. Take a look at Mark 16:8. This is where Mark probably finished writing his Gospel. Notice how the Gospel ends – on a note of paralyzing fear despite the good news of Jesus' resurrection. The abuse scandals that have exploded within the Church across the world are evidence of failed discipleship and paralyzed fearful leadership. Mark's Gospel is a challenge today to Jesus' disciples to follow him with courage no matter how painful the truth or how difficult the journey ahead.

Finally, this is a sombre Gospel because it deals in great detail with Jesus' death. Jesus, the Messiah, the Son of God, is also the Suffering Servant. God's love, made visible through Jesus' death, is a love that is vulnerable. Yet Mark proclaims that this vulnerable love will ultimately destroy evil and all human suffering.

This Gospel is no ugly duckling. It is magnificent and strong, and has much to say to us.

Second Sunday in Ordinary Time

15th January 2012

Preparing for Sunday

Read the Gospel: John 1:35-42

The explanation

Today's reading is from the Fourth Gospel because it tells of something not found in Mark's Gospel – namely, that some disciples of John the Baptizer begin to follow Jesus on the basis of John's own testimony. In the Synoptic Gospels, Jesus' first followers give up their previous occupation as fishermen in order to follow him. In the Fourth Gospel, they give up their commitment to John the Baptizer in order to follow Jesus. However, they do this on the basis of John's own witness. It is most probable that today's reading reflects the historical reality that some of John's disciples were among Jesus' first followers.

The Baptizer calls Jesus the "Lamb of God." He has used this title already (John 1:29). It is a phrase that is full of Old Testament imagery, particularly that of the Suffering Servant (Isaiah 53:7) and of the lamb used at the Passover meal. In using this rich title, John the Baptizer identifies Jesus as the Redeemer who will save the world from its sin. John now disappears from the text, having completed his role in giving witness to Jesus and in leading others to him.

The two former disciples of John now "follow" Jesus. The evangelist uses the verb "to follow" with two levels of meaning. First, it means literally to journey along with Jesus. Second, it means to be a disciple or "follower" of Jesus. Jesus' question to the two ("what are you looking for?") makes sense in the context of the storyline. At the more symbolic level his words question the disciples about what they are seeking in choosing to follow him. These are Jesus' first words in the Fourth Gospel. His question is addressed to the two disciples but it is also addressed to you, the reader of the Gospel.

The two have become Jesus' disciples as they now use the Hebrew title Rabbi (teacher) for him. They ask Jesus where he is "staying." Their question to him also operates at two levels. At the literal level, they simply want to know Jesus' address. But at the symbolic level the verb "to stay" is often used of the deep, intimate and permanent relationship between God and humanity. Jesus' invitation to them ("come and see") is an offer to see him with the eyes of faith and to enter into a deep relationship with him.

Up to this point the two disciples have remained anonymous. Now we learn the name of one of them – Andrew. He is introduced as the brother of Simon (Peter). In this way the evangelist introduces the call of Simon. It is Andrew who introduces Jesus to Simon as the "Messiah." The word "Messiah" comes from the Hebrew *mashiach*, which means the "Anointed One," and refers to the ancient Jewish practice of anointing kings and prophets with oil. The Old Testament was translated into Greek between the third and second centuries BC in a text that today is known as the Septuagint. When the evangelists and the other New Testament authors quote the Old Testament in their works, they always use the Septuagint. However, the Septuagint has no easy Greek equivalent for the Jewish concept expressed by the Hebrew word *mashiach*. The best equivalent is the Greek word *christós*, which literally means "greasy headed" or "covered in oil"! The title "Christ" is derived from *christós* and simply means "Messiah." Jewish people in the first century AD believed that the Messiah would be a powerful king who would destroy the Roman occupation of Palestine and rule over a united Israel. Andrew and the other disciples will have to learn that Jesus is not that kind of Messiah. According to the writer of the Fourth Gospel, Jesus changes Simon's name to Cephas (Peter) in the first meeting with him. This is very different to Matthew who locates this story well into Jesus' Galilean ministry (Matthew 16:18). This is a good example of how different evangelists use traditions about Jesus in diverse ways according to their theological purposes. The writer of the Fourth Gospel places the event here as a demonstration of Jesus' knowledge about Peter's future role and ministry in the Church.

Coming back for another look

Read the Gospel passage again later in the week and think about the following:

• Today's short reading contains three different names for Jesus – "Lamb of God," "Rabbi" and "Messiah." It seems that Jesus' disciples experienced him in different ways and gave witness accordingly. Perhaps it is because each one of them had their own expectations and needs where Jesus was concerned. You are Jesus' disciple. Spend a little time today thinking about your own favourite title for Jesus. What are your expectations of him? What are your needs which only he can meet?

COME
AND
SEE

Third Sunday in Ordinary Time

22nd January 2012

Preparing for Sunday
Read the Gospel: Mark 1:14-20

The explanation

Finally, we begin our systematic reading of Mark's Gospel! Mark has already told us who Jesus is (Mark 1:1-13). Now he tells us about Jesus' ministry in Galilee (Mark 1:14–8:30). Today's reading offers a summary of Jesus' preaching and tells of the call of his first disciples.

Jesus' ministry in Galilee begins after the arrest of John the Baptizer. The Greek text reads that John was "given up" – a phrase that suggests he was arrested violently or betrayed for the purpose of killing him. Mark will use this exact phrase later on to describe Jesus' arrest, scourging and crucifixion. While Mark does not follow up on what happens to John at this point, he will return to it later (Mark 6:14-29). However, the mention of John's arrest right now sounds a chilling and unsettling note – preaching the good news of God's Kingdom means ending up being "given up." It is what happened to John and it is what will happen to Jesus, too.

Jesus now begins to preach God's Kingdom and Mark offers us a summary of his message: "The time is fulfilled, and the Kingdom of God has come near; repent, and believe in the good news." I would like to explain each phrase of this message so that you can appreciate more fully what Jesus actually said to the people of Galilee and what he says to you today. "The time is fulfilled" refers back to the expectation of the prophets that God would free the people of Israel. About 600 years before Jesus was born the people of Israel had been enslaved in Babylon (modern Iraq) for about five decades (586–539 BC). One of the great prophets of that time, Isaiah of Babylon (Isaiah 40–55), proclaimed that a time would come when God would send the Messiah to free Israel from every form of slavery. Jesus proclaims that this "time" has now arrived with him.

The "Kingdom of God" that Jesus talks of is not a place. It is rather God's sovereignty or rule over people. In welcoming the Kingdom as proclaimed by Jesus, people accept the renewed relationship with God that Jesus offers. Jesus says that God's Kingdom "has come near." It is here already, but has not yet fully arrived. This already-but-not-yet nature of God's Kingdom is intriguing. God's rule is already here in Jesus, in renewed relationships with God, and it has begun to transform people. But it has not yet completed the transformation and renewal of the world. Jesus' disciples will have to work for the Kingdom's completion.

"Repent, and believe in the good news" is the final part of Jesus' message. The Greek word for repentance is *metánoia* and means a radical conversion or turning around of one's life. The New Testament Greek verb "to believe (in)" simply means "to put one's trust in something or someone." Finally, the term "good news" means the message that God will liberate humanity from every form of slavery, including evil (Satan) and death. So Jesus' message is: "Turn your life around, be converted and put your trust in God's power to set you free."

Mark's Jesus never rests. He is constantly on the move fulfilling his mission. Having announced the central message of that mission, Jesus now begins to call people to follow him, starting with four fishermen from near Capernaum, a small village on the northern shore of the Sea of Galilee. They are Simon, Andrew, James and John. In calling followers to join him Jesus sends a powerful signal that discipleship, faith and life in community are all linked together. For Jesus, it is not possible to reduce discipleship and faith to something "private." Rather, discipleship is lived with others in a community of faith. The four who are called are two pairs of brothers (Simon/Andrew and James/John). Jesus invites them to leave their natural family unit and join a new family unit in a community of relationships with God, Jesus and one another. Jesus' invitation is to "follow" him.

The Greek text says that Jesus called them to follow "behind" him. The message is clear: to be a disciple is to follow Jesus along his way. Mark likes to emphasize Jesus' power. So when Jesus exercises his power, things happen immediately. The four respond "immediately" to Jesus' call and their adventure of discipleship begins.

Coming back for another look

Read the Gospel passage again later in the week and think about the following:

•   During the 2011 Irish General Election campaign, a politician was being interviewed on a phone-in show. One caller asked him a question about his religious belief. He refused to deal with the question on the grounds that religion was a "private matter." Secularists certainly would like to have it that way and keep religious faith "private" or "invisible." What do think of that? For Jesus "private" or "invisible" discipleship is meaningless. Your discipleship and mine only have meaning in belonging to a community of faith that follows Jesus along his way.

Fourth Sunday in Ordinary Time

29th January 2012

Preparing for Sunday
Read the Gospel: Mark 1:21-28

The explanation

There were many individual stories about Jesus in circulation before Mark ever wrote his Gospel. Most of these tell of events that happened in Galilee and they probably originated there. Many involve miracles. The term "miracle story" is one that tells of some powerful deed performed by Jesus. They are usually divided into three types: healing stories, exorcism stories and nature miracles, such as the multiplication of food.

Today's reading tells of Jesus' first miracle, an exorcism, which happens on a Saturday in the synagogue in Capernaum. The synagogue was one of the most important religious institutions in Jesus' day. The word "synagogue" comes from the Greek *synagogē* and simply means "assembly." The Hebrew term is *beyt knesset* ("house of assembly") or even *beyt ha-midrash* ("house of teaching"). In Galilee in the first century AD every town and village had its synagogue. It was a place for prayer, worship and instruction in the Jewish faith. Jesus' strategy for preaching God's Kingdom took him throughout Galilee from synagogue to synagogue, teaching and preaching. The reaction to Jesus' teaching by those in the synagogue is one of amazement. His teaching is so powerfully authoritative that it eclipses that of the scribes. These were the local theologians or scripture scholars who offered regular teaching based on their interpretation of the sacred texts. If the crowd present are amazed at Jesus' teaching, they are even more amazed at his exorcism miracle.

Mark places the story of the exorcism between these two reactions of amazement. The man with the unclean spirit cries out in response to Jesus' teaching and in recognition of his presence. He calls Jesus by name. In the Jewish culture of the time, when one person called another by name the one doing the calling was seen to have authority over the one called. The unclean spirit not only calls Jesus by his public name (Jesus of Nazareth) but also by his true identity (Holy One of God). So in terms of the cultural understanding of that time, the unclean spirit should have defeated Jesus. Yet this does not happen because ultimately God's power working through Jesus is victorious. It can easily silence the spirit and drive it out of the man. As always with Mark, Jesus' power has immediate effect. The agonized response of the spirit is seen in the convulsions of the man. As the spirit departs, it gives a "loud cry" of defeat and protest as its power over the man is now ended. On Golgotha Jesus too will give a "loud cry" as he dies on the cross, and the power of evil will think it a moment in which God's Kingdom is destroyed. But Jesus' cry will be one of victory over evil.

As they did with Jesus' teaching, the crowd are amazed at the miracle which is described as a "teaching" that has authority over unclean spirits. For Mark, both Jesus' teaching and his exorcism are signs of the closeness of God's Kingdom. Both are actions of liberation whereby Jesus frees people from enslavement.

This story also emphasizes the difference between Jesus' teaching and that of the scribes. Scribal teaching is based on the study and interpretation of the scriptures. Jesus' teaching is based on the rule of God. In this way the exorcism is a miracle that gives effect to Jesus' teaching. Scribal teaching has failed to free the man from that which enslaved him. It is only Jesus, who is the presence and power of God, who ultimately frees him. For Mark, this miracle proclaims that a new era has begun with Jesus and that the enslavement to evil (Satan) will be ended. The response of the people is simply one of questioning amazement. They do not recognize fully who Jesus is and what his presence means. Nonetheless, his fame spreads throughout Galilee.

Coming back for another look

Read the Gospel passage again later in the week and think about the following:

• It is not possible to identify precisely the type of "demon" that enslaved the man in the synagogue. Some scholars think it was some form of emotional or mental illness. While we Christians do not attribute physical or mental illness to demons, we do know that sickness and healing have their spiritual dimensions. Sometimes it is easier to blame traumatic afflictions on demons or even on God than face the struggle and fear associated with illness. Today's reading invites us to trust in God's loving care, even when in the midst of sickness it seems remote.

Fifth Sunday in Ordinary Time

5th February 2012

Preparing for Sunday
Read the Gospel: Mark 1:29-39

The explanation

People in Jesus' day understood physical illness in terms of demonic power. So Jesus' cure of Simon's mother-in-law is yet another demonstration of his authority over evil. Jesus has just left the synagogue and now enters the house of his two new friends (Simon and Andrew) along with James and John. Simon and Andrew "tell him about her," but probably were not expecting a miracle. Perhaps they tell him about her since there is nobody to get a meal ready for them because she is in bed with a fever!

Jesus goes to the woman and takes her by the hand. Respected rabbis in Jesus' day would never have done such a thing and certainly not on the Sabbath. They would have avoided touching a sick person, not just out of fear of getting an illness, but also of being made ritually unclean and so temporarily isolated from the rest of the believing community. But Jesus does not catch an illness or uncleanness. Rather the woman "catches" a healing from Jesus. The fever flees in the presence of Jesus' power, just as the unclean spirit did in the synagogue earlier that day.

Once healed, she begins to offer them hospitality. Again it is important to look at the Greek text. It says that she began "to offer service" to Jesus and his friends. The Greek word for service is *diakonía*, and is one of Mark's key concepts in the Gospel. Jesus will later describe his mission in terms of service (Mark 10:45). Towards the end of the Gospel, at Golgotha, the women who stand there are those who had "followed him and served him" (Mark

15:40-41). At the beginning and at the end of the Gospel Mark offers a portrait of women who, not just offered hospitality to Jesus, but also shared in his ministry. Simon's mother-in-law becomes the first woman disciple to do so and she will not be the last.

It would be easy to miss the point when reading this short miracle story. It reminds us that in Jesus' new family of disciples there was a place both for the ministry of his male *and* female disciples. While Mark's story focuses on Simon's mother-in-law, it tells us nothing about Simon's wife. However, we are indebted to Paul who tells us that Simon's wife also ministered alongside her famous husband (1 Corinthians 9:5).

The cure of the man with the unclean spirit and of Simon's mother-in-law takes place on a Saturday. Once the Sabbath ends (at sundown) all who need healing make for Simon's house. They are physically sick (like Simon's mother-in-law) and possessed (like the man in the synagogue). Mark tells us that Jesus was so popular that the entire city was gathered at the door of Simon's house! Typically, Mark likes to use exaggerated speech when giving brief summaries. Jesus powerfully silences the demons as their speech risks distorting the message of God's Kingdom.

On Sunday morning Jesus leaves Capernaum for a deserted place to pray. Everything that has happened the day before was by the power of God. So it is natural for Jesus now to turn to God in prayer. His popularity, based on the previous day's miracles, has triggered huge enthusiasm and he needs to distance himself from it in order to continue his mission. But his time of prayer is short lived as his new friends "hunt him down." Whenever Mark uses this expression, it always has a negative ring to it. Since the disciples fail to understand Jesus' need for time apart in prayer, they intrude. It is the first in a long series of failures by them.

Jesus now decides to move on to preach in other towns, for this is what he "came out to do." The phrase is puzzling. Where did Jesus come out from – Nazareth or Capernaum or even from God? Jesus may well be signalling that his mission is God-directed. However, like the disciples, we are left to think over what he might mean. Today's reading ends with a summary of Jesus' mission in Galilee. He has set himself against the power of evil by proclaiming God's Kingdom.

Coming back for another look

Read the Gospel passage again later in the week and think about the following:

• It is important to remember that God never wills a human being to suffer in any way. Jesus is presented in the reading as having power over illness and pain. He will have to face his own suffering and death at Golgotha, while still placing complete trust in God. This is not an easy path.

Sixth Sunday in Ordinary Time

12th February 2012

Preparing for Sunday
Read the Gospel: Mark 1:40-45

The explanation

Today's reading is about Jesus' cure of a leper. Leprosy, or Hansen's disease, did not exist in Palestine in Old Testament times. There is increasing evidence to suggest that it began to appear by the first century AD. Mark uses the Greek word *leprós* to describe the man. It means a person with any kind of scaly, contagious skin disease. Such a person was considered ritually unclean and was isolated from the community until the condition was cured. The leper in today's reading clearly has faith in Jesus. He breaks out of his social and religious isolation to come to Jesus because he believes that Jesus can cure him, if Jesus should choose to do so.

Jesus' reaction is most interesting. In order to understand it, I would like to tell you something about the text of Mark's Gospel. We do not have the original copy of Mark's text. All we have is a manuscript which is a copy of other manuscripts made over two to six centuries after Mark wrote his Gospel. There are many of these manuscripts and they do not all agree on the precise text of Mark. Biblical scholars have had to study all these manuscripts in order to come up with what, in all probability, is the closest text to Mark's original. In terms of Jesus' reaction, many manuscripts read that Jesus was "moved with pity," offering a comforting portrait of Jesus. However, other manuscripts read that he was "moved with anger." It is very likely that over time more difficult readings were touched up to be more reasonable. This may well have happened here, where the more difficult portrait of an angry Jesus is replaced with the easier portrait of a compassionate Jesus. Most translations today follow the easier and softer reading. But I am going to follow the more difficult reading as it is the one supported by the best manuscripts available.

So why is Jesus angry? At this man who has broken the Jewish law and approached him? At the man's questioning of his willingness to heal? At the way the man is enslaved and ravaged by a horrible (demonic) disease? Jesus wants to help this man but it will be at a cost. The consequence of the healing for Jesus will mean celebrity status and a popular superficial understanding of his mission.

ISOLATED - ALONE - FORGOTTEN!

His miracles are meant to show the presence of God's power. They are an invitation to people to recognize his power and to listen to his message. If people only see him as a celebrity wonder-worker, they will misunderstand him and his mission. Nonetheless, Jesus touches the leper and speaks the words of healing. He restores the man both to health and to his place in the community of Israel by both touch and word. The miracle is as immediate as it is effective.

But Jesus is still angry. The English text reads: "moved with anger, he sent him away." The Greek text uses more forceful language. Mark uses a very rare New Testament word here to describe Jesus' mood. He describes Jesus as "snorting like a horse with inward rage." More than that, Jesus does not just send the man away; he "thrusts" him away. Jesus warns the man to keep quiet about the miracle in the hope that it will not distract from his mission. He orders the man to fulfil the requirements of the Jewish Law so as to end his social and religious isolation.

However, the warning has no effect. The man tells everyone everywhere about the miracle and Jesus becomes a celebrity. He now has to avoid the urban areas, living in the country, while the crowds keep coming. There is a deep irony here. The leper lived in isolation because of his disease. Jesus now lives in isolation because of his cure. The cost to Jesus is high. His power to heal has triggered popular enthusiasm and made him famous. In time this will lead to jealousy on the part of the authorities and to his ultimate isolation on the cross at Golgotha.

Coming back for another look

Read the Gospel passage again later in the week and think about the following:

• The leper lived in social and religious isolation. Today it is easy for us to isolate people who have AIDS or some other frightening disease. We probably are scared to touch such people. People can even stop visiting a dying family member or friend, causing devastating isolation. This Gospel reading shows Jesus rescuing a man from isolation by befriending and touching him.

Seventh Sunday in Ordinary Time

19th February 2012

Preparing for Sunday

Read the Gospel: Mark 2:1-12

The explanation

The "controversy story" is another feature of Jesus' Galilean ministry in Mark's Gospel. This is a story in which Jesus engages with the Jewish religious authorities who criticize him for his actions but he always wins the argument by turning the tables on his critics. Mark 2:1–3:6 contains five controversy stories. Today's reading is the first of these – a controversy over Jesus' authority to forgive sins.

Jesus is back in Capernaum again and has been living quietly in a house there. Mark does not say exactly which house but it is most likely Simon's. Very quickly, the word spreads. As with the healing of Simon's mother-in-law, so many people gather at the house that they are forced to crowd around the door. Jesus begins to preach, but is soon interrupted. Some people bring a paralyzed man to him but because of the crowd they cannot get to him.

Palestinian houses at that time had roofs made from wooden crossbeams laid across stone walls and covered with thatch and straw. The four people

carrying the paralyzed man take him up on to the roof, make a hole in it, and let the man down on a stretcher right before Jesus. Some biblical commentators argue that Mark's Greek word for the stretcher (*krábattos*) suggests that the immobile man is very poor.

Jesus sees "their faith." The four men have gone to great lengths to get their paralyzed friend to Jesus. In fact, they have shown such a depth of faith that it moves Jesus, and he assures the paralyzed man that his sins are forgiven, triggering the controversy.

Suddenly Mark tells us that there are scribes present and they react negatively but secretly. This is the beginning of the hostile relationship between Jesus and the scribes which will ultimately bring him to Golgotha. Yet in this first moment of the conflict, not a single word is uttered.

For the scribes, Jesus is blaspheming because he is claiming for himself the power to forgive sins which is something only God can do. Yet Jesus is powerful and he knows what the scribes are thinking. He challenges them to choose between what is easier for him to do – to proclaim or speak the words of forgiveness of the man's sins or to command the cure of his paralysis. From the scribes' point of view, it is much easier to speak the words of forgiveness because nobody will see their effect. But anyone claiming to forgive sins has to be a blasphemer since only God has such power. But if Jesus shows himself to have such power, then the scribes must face the reality of who he is. Jesus is prepared to work the miracle both to heal the paralyzed man and to establish his authority for all to see.

Jesus refers to himself as the "Son of Man." What does this title mean? You will have to continue to read Mark to understand it. For the moment just note that this is how Jesus refers to himself and that as "Son of Man" he has divine power to forgive sins. Mark wants you to remember the story, the title and the authority he claims. Mark wants you to accept simply that Jesus is the "Son of Man" and let the meaning of this title unfold as you read further.

Jesus now does the more difficult thing as a demonstration of his power. He commands the cure by ordering the man to stand up and to walk home free of disease. The miracle happens "immediately." Once again Jesus' authority is obvious. His power to work the visible miracle (the physical cure) is proof of his authority to work the invisible miracle (the forgiveness of sins). In this way Jesus shows that forgiveness of sins is not something that falls from heaven. Rather, it is offered by Jesus who is the healing and reconciling presence of God. His power is seen by all and it generates amazement. However, the scribes remain silent and seem to disappear from the story. Those who speak out praise God for what has been done through Jesus, the "Son of Man" – whatever this title might mean.

Coming back for another look

Read the Gospel passage again later in the week and think about the following:

- Jesus' first miracles have rescued people from isolation. In this reading he saves a man from sin, which can separate people from God. It is easy for us to isolate those we label "sinners." God, whose reconciling and forgiving love is present in Jesus, will have none of this.

Why does this man speak that way?

the son of Man
has authority
on earth to
forgive sins

Your sins are forgiven,

who can forgive sins
but God alone?

We have never seen anything like this

Springtime
New Life

The Season of Lent

The Season of Lent is the forty-day period of preparation for Easter that begins on Ash Wednesday, which is a moveable feast determined by the date of Easter. This year Ash Wednesday falls on February 22nd. Originally this season was called *Tessarakostē*, which is the Greek for "fortieth day (before Easter)." Eventually this Greek term was translated into Latin as *Quadragesima*. Many modern languages preserve this word as *Quaresima* (Italian), *Cuaresma* (Spanish), *Quaresma* (Portuguese) and even as *Carghas* (Irish). By the eleventh century AD sermons began to be preached in various local languages, while the rest of the liturgy continued to be celebrated in Latin. In Northern European preaching, *Quadragesima* began to be referred to as *Lenz* in German and as *Lencten* in Old English. These are words for Spring and refer to the noticeable lengthening of springtime days. Our English word "Lent" comes from such words.

Officially, Lent is the forty-day period from Ash Wednesday to Holy Thursday, excluding its six Sundays which continue to be celebrations of the Lord's resurrection. Good Friday and Holy Saturday are not part of Lent, but are linked with Easter Sunday in what is known as the Easter Triduum.

Lent is a time of preparation for the celebration of Holy Week and the Easter Triduum. This preparation consists of prayer, penitence, charity and self-denial. As with Advent, the liturgical colour for Lent is purple. The only exception is on the Fourth Sunday of Lent, which is known as *Laetare* Sunday, for which the colour is rose (as with Gaudete Sunday in Advent). The Latin word *laetare* means "rejoice with" and since the Mass begins with the words of the prophet Isaiah – "Rejoice with (*laetare*) Jerusalem, and be glad for her, all you who love her ..." (Isaiah 66:10-11) – the Sunday came to be known as *Laetare* Sunday. This is the midpoint of Lent and the colour rose symbolizes the anticipated joy of the Resurrection breaking into the sombre and penitential Lenten season. *Laetare* Sunday eventually became a day on which fasting was relaxed. People made special Easter cakes and gave them as gifts to their mothers. In time, *Laetare* Sunday became "Mother's Day," which is still the case in Ireland and the UK.

Lent is also the season when non-baptized adults

who wish to become Catholics are prepared for their baptism at the Easter Vigil. This process of Christian initiation has largely determined the themes and the Gospel texts for the Sundays of Lent. In Year B these texts are taken from the Gospels of Mark and of John. On the First Sunday of Lent we read an account of Jesus' temptation, which reminds us that life as Christians will have its trials and struggles. Jesus' transfiguration dominates the Second Sunday of Lent, offering us a glimpse of his power and glory and gives us hope. The Third Sunday of Lent presents the account of Jesus' angry cleansing of the Jerusalem Temple and his call for radical discipleship. On *Laetare* Sunday we hear Jesus tell his would-be disciple Nicodemus of God's passionate desire to save everyone. On the Fifth Sunday of Lent we hear Jesus talk about the meaning of his approaching death. The Gospel reading on Passion (Palm) Sunday is always taken from one of the Synoptic Passion Narratives. This year we read Mark's account.

As Lent begins and you make your choices on how to prepare for Easter, it would be good to review how you have been using this book and its programme of reflection. If you have been using it fairly regularly and well, please continue to do so. If you have given up on reading each Sunday's Gospel, perhaps you could take up the task again and make this a central part of your Lenten practice. The Gospel has much to say to you in this season

and it will bring you well prepared to celebrate Holy Week and the Easter Triduum with renewed commitment and faith.

The Year of the Suffering Servant

First Sunday of Lent

26th February 2012

Preparing for Sunday

Read the Gospel: Mark 1:12-15

The explanation

You have come across most of today's reading already. Mark's story of Jesus' testing in the wilderness follows immediately on the account of Jesus' baptism, which you read previously for the feast of the Baptism of the Lord. It would be helpful for you now to go back and re-read the explanation for Mark 1:7-11 given on pages 32-33 above. Today's text also precedes the account of Jesus' proclamation of God's Kingdom, which forms part of the Gospel reading for the Third Sunday in Ordinary Time, which again you have read already. I suggest that you go back and re-read the explanation for Mark 1:14-15 given on pages 40-41 above.

The part of the text that is new is Mark 1:12-13 which deals with what is traditionally called the "temptation" of Jesus. Mark is the first to tell this story in an account that is brief and succinct. The later Synoptic writers offer longer and more detailed accounts (Matthew 4:1-11 and Luke 4:1-13).

The traditional description for today's story is the "temptation of Jesus." However, the same verb is used in New Testament Greek for both "tempt" and "test." So we must ask if, according to Mark, Jesus is "tempted" or "tested." There is no doubt that in Matthew's and Luke's accounts Jesus is tempted because the devil proposes three seductive possibilities to him that are false and completely at odds with his identity as the Son of God. Since this does not happen in Mark's account, it might be more appropriate to think of Jesus being tested rather than tempted. There are many biblical examples of people being tested by God – Abraham, Job, Moses, and even Israel itself. In fact, the forty-year desert trek through the wilderness becomes a place of testing for Israel before it can settle in the Promised Land. In these examples people are placed in extreme situations, without much support or resources, so that their readiness to follow God's call can be evaluated and purified. This is the most likely background to Mark's account of Jesus' testing which is brought about by the Holy Spirit. Mark's description of this is forceful: "the Spirit immediately drove him out into the wilderness." The strength of the language emphasizes the extremity of the environment Jesus is now brought into.

"Forty days" is a favourite biblical unit of time. The Great Flood lasted forty days, as did Moses' sojourn on Mount Sinai. The prophet Elijah fled through the wilderness for a similar period of time. "Forty days" is a biblical way of representing a long period of time. Mark tells us that Jesus was in the wilderness for a similar biblical period of extended time.

Mark also adds two other details. He tells us that Jesus was "with the wild beasts" and that "angels waited on him." The reference to the wild animals underscores the extreme and hostile environment in which Jesus finds himself. Judeans of the first century AD would have regarded the wilderness as the haunt of dangerous animals and evil spirits. Jesus' presence in such a place highlights the intense vulnerability of his situation.

Mark's second detail, about the angels who offer Jesus *diakonía* or service, is a counterpart to the danger he is in. Even though the environment is extreme and menacing, God offers care and protection to his Son in the form of the angels' ministry.

But this is not the end of Jesus' testing in desolate environments. Jesus' ultimate testing will begin with his sorrow in Gethsemane and it will end with his cry of anguish from the cross at Golgotha. Mark's account of Jesus' testing is the shortest among the Synoptic writers. It may be that Mark is less interested in describing the testing of Jesus as in emphasizing that he enjoys God's protection and intimacy as the Beloved Son who remains faithful.

Coming back for another look

Read the Gospel again later in the week and think about the following:

• Jesus' preparation for his mission and ministry involves entrusting himself radically to God. The story of his testing is a reminder that God is always with us, no matter how fearsome the "beasts" that life can bring our way. Trusting God as Jesus did is not only a key element of our discipleship but essential for any intimate relationship with God.

Second Sunday of Lent

4th March 2012

Preparing for Sunday
Read the Gospel: Mark 9:2-10

The explanation

One of the most sombre parts of Mark's stark Gospel is the section dealing with Jesus' journey from Galilee to Jerusalem (Mark 8:31–10:52). I will tell you more about this journey later. Suffice to say that it is not an easy journey for Jesus or his disciples. But one of the moments of relief on the journey is the transfiguration of Jesus, which is told in today's reading. Mark doesn't identify where it happens, other than to say it was "a high mountain apart." One possibility is Mount Hermon, the imposing and often snow-capped mountain that dominates the borders of Israel and Lebanon. But the traditional identification of the mountain is with Mount Tabor, which is 18km west of the Sea of Galilee and is the only high mountain standing alone in Lower Galilee.

In the presence of the three disciples Jesus is changed in some way. The Greek text says that he underwent a "metamorphosis" or transformation. This change involves a particularly brilliant whiteness of his clothes, beyond any human capacity to produce. In the Bible brilliant whiteness is associated with heaven, while metamorphosis was a process whereby a person's inner self was displayed outwardly. Putting these two ideas together, the text is saying that Jesus was changed in a way by which his divinity was outwardly revealed to the three disciples for the first time.

The appearance of Moses and Elijah is not easy to interpret and there are many scholarly theories. The Jewish Bible of that time consisted of two parts, (the Law and the Prophets), symbolized here by Moses and Elijah. Accordingly, Jesus, God's Messiah and Beloved Son, is the fulfilment of the hopes and prophecies of the Jewish scriptures. Another theory is based on what Elijah, Moses and Jesus have in common. They spoke with God atop high mountains. As they now stand on either side of the transfigured Jesus, their presence affirms God's power working through him.

Yet Peter fails to recognize Jesus' identity. His use of the title "rabbi" suggests he sees Jesus merely as another Jewish teacher. His declaration ("it is good for us to be here") is inappropriately low-key and

Mount Hermon

his desire to pitch three tents underscores his ignorance of what is being offered to him and to his companions. He still sees Jesus simply as another good and holy figure and not as Messiah and Son of God. His desire to freeze the moment and not continue the journey to Jerusalem illustrates that he has not understand all that Jesus has been saying up to this point. Mark explains Peter's ignorance and confusion on the basis that he and his companions were terrified. Fear and its destructive effect on discipleship are themes to which Mark will return repeatedly right to the Gospel's original conclusion (Mark 16:8).

Now God speaks and corrects Peter's inadequate understanding. Jesus is not just another rabbi or even another biblical figure. He is God's Son. The three disciples are not to set up tents. They are to "listen" to Jesus, even if they do not fully understand him. Above all, they are to listen to what he is saying about suffering and dying. Jesus is God's Beloved Son, as Isaac was Abraham's. Abraham did not sacrifice his beloved son (Genesis 22:1-19); yet God will do so to save humankind. The transfiguration story is not simply about revealing Jesus' identity as Beloved Son. It is also about God's revelation of the cost of saving the world through

The Year of the Suffering Servant

the suffering and death of the Beloved Son.

Once God has spoken, the vision ends and the heavenly figures disappear. "Only Jesus" remains and he is as he was before. Yet everything is different. We know that God's Beloved Son will continue his journey to Jerusalem where he will suffer and die to save the world. Jesus warns his disciples to remain quiet about their experience until after the Resurrection. Jesus' power and glory are not to be separated from what awaits him in Jerusalem and can only be understood in that context. There will be no Easter glory without Golgotha's cross.

Coming back for another look

Read the Gospel again later in the week and think about the following:

• Jesus died a cruel death, in immense weakness and pain, in order to save us. As Risen Lord, he is infinitely powerful in word and deed. There is no Easter glory without Golgotha's cross. By his wounds we have been healed. It is not easy to put all these statements about Jesus together. Like the three disciples on the mountain, we can be confused and disoriented as we struggle to make sense of Jesus. We can do no better than that which they were told to do: to listen to him who is God's Beloved Son.

Third Sunday of Lent

11th March 2012

Preparing for Sunday
Read the Gospel: John 2:13-25

The explanation

Today we read John's account of the cleansing of the Temple. The story is also found in the Synoptic Gospels, which locate the event in Jerusalem during the *final week of Jesus' life*. The Fourth Gospel locates it at the *beginning of Jesus' ministry*. This is yet another example of how the evangelists use the same tradition differently according to their own perspectives. The Synoptic evangelists present Jesus' anti-Temple protest in Jerusalem as that which triggers the reaction of the authorities and ultimately brings him to the cross. John the Evangelist uses the tradition differently. At Cana Jesus has revealed the new life he offers (John 2:1-11). His action in the Temple highlights the threat presented to this new life by the old religious order, symbolized by the Temple.

Which tradition is the more historical? It is extremely unlikely that the Jewish authorities would have tolerated such confrontational activity by Jesus at the beginning of his ministry and would have moved against him promptly. For this reason biblical scholarship tends to regard the Synoptic chronology as the most historically accurate.

John's description of Jesus is dramatic. Armed with a whip Jesus drives animals and people out of the Temple court, scattering money and overturning tables as he goes. If you are going to understand fully what Jesus' action is about, you will need to put the scene into its proper context. Animals were required for sacrifice by law. The city was full of Passover pilgrims. These would need to buy animals for the Temple sacrifice and to pay the Temple tax. Roman and Greek coins used the image of the emperor and declared him a god. Pious Jews simply could not use such currency for religious purposes. So Roman and Greek money needed to be changed into Temple currency. In short, both the animals and the moneychangers were essential for the Temple liturgy. For Jesus, this system of sacrifice had reduced God's Temple to a marketplace and in condemning it Jesus challenges the power of the Temple authorities. John's account quotes Psalm 69:10 and modifies it slightly as "Zeal for your house will consume me." In this way John links Jesus' action against the Temple with his passion and death, when he will be "consumed" by the crucifixion.

Those who witness Jesus' action demand that he produce authorization to act in such a provocative manner. Jesus' response is to talk about the destruction and rebuilding of the Temple. Herod the Great had begun rebuilding the Temple in 19 BC and it would continue until 64 AD. If the reference to 46 years of construction is historically accurate, it would suggest a date of 27 AD for Jesus' action in the Temple, which is a plausible date for the beginnings of his ministry. But his questioners have misunderstood him. Jesus is not talking about rebuilding the Temple. He is talking about the resurrection of the "temple of his body." For the Jews the Temple was the place of God's presence on earth. For Jesus' followers the place of God's presence on earth will be Jesus' risen body. Only after the Resurrection will his actions and words be remembered through the power of the Holy Spirit whom Jesus will send.

In contrast with those who challenge him, many others in Jerusalem believe in Jesus because of his miracles. Yet miracles are always problematic. People who want only miracles can easily reject Jesus' message. He is mistrustful of this and the Greek text expresses it pithily. In Greek the same verb is used for "believe" and "entrust." The Greek text states that Jesus did not believe in their belief in him! His mistrust of their faith is based on his own deep knowledge of human nature.

Coming back for another look

Read the Gospel again later in the week and think about the following:

- How do you make sense of the fact that Jesus got angry?
- The crucifixion is the sign of how seriously Jesus took his faith. He got so angry at evil that evil got angry with him and tried to destroy him. His cross is the symbol of his healthy reforming anger and the cost of it. It is the kind of healthy reforming anger that leads us to face up to sinful evil, indifference, corruption and dulled faith. In the Temple and in the Church.

Fourth Sunday of Lent (Laetare Sunday)

18th March 2012

Preparing for Sunday
Read the Gospel: John 3:14-21

The explanation

Today's Gospel doesn't make for light reading or simple interpretation. It consists of part of a speech Jesus gives following a conversation with a man called Nicodemus. Read John 3:1-2a in order to understand the context. Nicodemus is a Jewish leader and a Pharisee who seeks out Jesus. But he does it in secret, at night, under the cover of darkness. Night is often used in the Fourth Gospel to symbolize separation from the presence of God. Nicodemus is a would-be disciple but still has some way to go before he reaches full discipleship. In John 3:2b-10 Nicodemus asks questions and Jesus gives answers. In John 3:11-21 Jesus' answers develops into a full-blown theological discourse or speech. Today's reading is taken from that lengthy discourse, and has to do with the way in which the "Son of Man" will be "lifted up." Jesus refers back to an episode from the Old Testament when Moses saved the people of Israel from serpents by "lifting up" a bronze serpent on a pole. All who were bitten and looked at the bronze serpent were saved (Numbers 21:4-9).

"Lifting up" has two meanings in the Fourth Gospel. It can refer to Jesus being lifted up on the cross at Golgotha. Or it can mean the glorification or exaltation of Jesus. John's theology of the cross is quite different from that of the other evangelists. Central to John's theology is that Jesus is exalted by means of the crucifixion. As John sees it, Jesus' crucifixion, resurrection and ascension are all a single event. Just as the bronze serpent on the pole gave life to the people of Israel in the wilderness, Jesus on the cross will give eternal life to those who believe. Again John is trying to communicate something quite complex. Eternal life is not just something in the future after death. Eternal life begins here and now and is life lived in the unending presence of the eternal God.

John's community in the first century AD had a very strong sense of those who belonged to it and those who were opposed to it. This is reflected in the theology of the Fourth Gospel. For John, Jesus is God's gift to the world, given in love for all the people of the world without distinction. Yet people are going to have to make a choice in relation to this wonderful gift. If people choose to believe in Jesus, then they become children of God and receive the gift of eternal life, beginning here and now. On the other hand, if people choose not to believe in Jesus, then the gift of eternal life will not be available to them. Jesus' very presence challenges the world to make a decision about him. Those who choose him are saved. Those who do not are condemned.

The final part of Jesus' speech uses images of light and darkness which are favourite themes in the Fourth Gospel. A person is not good or bad in some predetermined way. It is only in their faith-response to Jesus that someone is revealed as good or bad. Nicodemus has not yet come to belief. He remains in the darkness of night until he can come to faith in Jesus. As I said above, this text does not make for light reading or easy interpretation.

Coming back for another look

Read the Gospel again later in the week and think about the following:

- This is a text you must read with care because it offers a challenging invitation from Jesus. It is a demanding invitation because, if you accept it, you will have to open yourself to the consequences. One consequence is that you choose to believe firmly that Jesus is God's Son and that God loves you and the rest of humanity so much that God gave Jesus as a gift to the world and to you. The

other consequence is that you fully acknowledge that God's love for you is never-ending and that God asks you to accept the gift of Jesus. All the language in the Gospel reading about belief and unbelief, saved and condemned, light and darkness, simply emphasizes how serious God is in offering you the gift of Jesus.

Fifth Sunday of Lent

25 March 2012

Preparing for Sunday
Read the Gospel: John 12:20-33

The explanation

Today's Gospel is one of the most important texts in the Fourth Gospel for interpreting the significance of Jesus' death. As with last Sunday's, it doesn't make for light reading. Traditionally, the Church has used three different models to understand the meaning of Jesus' death. The first understands his death as an act of ransom, or payment, to God by which Jesus bought the world freedom from evil and death. The second views Jesus' death as a sacrifice offered to God in atonement for human sin. The third model understands his death as a morally good deed which reveals the depth of God's love for us. Today's Gospel story offers a powerfully different model for understanding his death.

The story opens with the arrival of some "Greeks." They are Greek-speaking Gentiles who are interested in Judaism and are on their way to Jerusalem for the Passover festival. They want to "see" Jesus. The Greek text implies that they want to become his disciples. Their request marks a new development in Jesus'

ministry as his group of followers extends beyond Jewish people to include Gentiles. This will be the Church's future. It will move beyond Jerusalem and Judaism to embrace the whole world. But this can only happen when Jesus, the "Son of Man," is "glorified" through his death, resurrection and return to the Father. In short, the arrival of the Greeks anticipates a future Church of Jews and Gentiles but also points the way to Jesus' death. The rest of today's text is taken up with Jesus' own interpretation of his death.

The first image he uses is of a seed. He uses it to interpret his death, not to talk about the resurrection of the body. The key to understanding his teaching is to be found in the difference between the seed which "remains just a single grain" and the seed which, in dying, "bears much fruit." Jesus says that his death will be fruitful because it will give life to a whole community of believers which will be gathered in his name. Later in today's text Jesus restates the meaning of his parable in explicit language – "and I, when I am lifted up from the earth, will draw all people to myself."

He then talks about those who "love" and "hate" their life. Those who love their life are those who are unable to give that life in service for others and so put

moment in Biblical literature. The Father says that he has glorified his own name in everything Jesus has said and done up to now and that he will glorify it again in all that will befall Jesus in the "hour." Those present are not sure what they hear. Some say it's thunder while others maintain it's an angel's voice. In the Old Testament, thunder and angelic voices were always understood as signs of God's presence. So while the crowd knows that God has revealed something, they fail to recognize God's very presence in Jesus. Finally, Jesus returns to the theme of judgement. How the world responds to him in his "hour" when he is "lifted up" (crucified and glorified) will constitute judgement. God offers salvation without limit to all people through Jesus. How people respond to that offer is up to them.

Coming back for another look

Read the Gospel again later in the week and think about the following:

•   The Fourth Gospel understands the meaning of Jesus' death in terms of reconciliation between God and humanity. It is not reconciliation based on ransom or atoning sacrifice but on the restoration of relationship. By dying Jesus creates a believing community of love and service through which all people are offered a restored relationship with God and the gift of eternal life. However, it is essential that people believe in Jesus if they want to receive his gift.

themselves outside the Christian community. Those who "hate their life in this world" are those who follow Jesus' example and so are able to receive the gift of eternal life. They will be honoured by the Father for their love and service.

The second image Jesus uses is that of his "hour." This is the Fourth Gospel's preferred word to describe his agony and death. Jesus will not avoid what awaits him but will embrace it in his love for the Father, who now speaks. This is always a rare but hugely significant

Palm Sunday

1 April 2012

Preparing for Sunday
Read the Gospel: Mark 14:1–15:47

The explanation

During Holy Week we listen to two accounts of the passion of Jesus. On Good Friday the passion narrative is always taken from the Fourth Gospel. On Passion Sunday the passion narrative is always taken from one of the Synoptic Gospels. Today we read Mark's account. I'm not going to summarize the story. It's best if you read it slowly and follow the dialogues and the drama for yourself. However, I will tell you what makes Mark's passion narrative unique by outlining two of its main characteristics. The first is the issue of Jesus' identity, which as we know is crucial for Mark. So it will come as no surprise to discover that it dominates his passion narrative. For Mark, Jesus is the "Son of God" and Israel's Suffering "Messiah" or "Christ." On the journey from Galilee to Jerusalem Jesus attempts three times to explain the concept of a suffering Messiah to his disciples but they completely misunderstand him. Mark also tells us that Jesus used the title "Son of Man" of himself. With all this in mind, pay particular attention to Jesus' trial before the Jewish authorities. It is at this trial that the titles "Christ" ("Messiah), "Son of God" and "Son of Man" are brought together with clarity. Jesus, who called himself "Son of Man," is finally revealed as both the Son of God and Israel's Messiah (Mark 14:60-62).

Watch out also for the issue of Jesus' identity in his trial before Pontius Pilate (Mark 15:2-15). Pilate asks if Jesus is the "King of the Jews." The title is ambiguous. In political terms it means a Jewish ruler who would challenge the authority of Tiberius Caesar in Judea. In Jewish religious terms it means Israel's Messiah. Jesus' silence can be interpreted to suggest that he accepts the title in religious terms but rejects it in political terms.

There is another Roman soldier in Mark's passion narrative who is the hero of the Gospel. He is the centurion who stands on Golgotha and sees the way Jesus dies and then confesses Jesus' identity as God's Son. The revelation of Jesus' identity in the passion narrative takes place only in the context of his suffering and death. Only when his disciples recognize Jesus as the one who suffered, died and was raised again can they profess their belief in him as Son of God and Messiah. After his death and resurrection, there is no longer any doubt about his identity. That is why Mark can profess Jesus' identity unambiguously at the beginning of the Gospel (Mark 1:1).

A second characteristic of Mark's passion narrative is the disciples' lack of understanding. They have failed to appreciate both his identity and destiny throughout his mission in Galilee. On the journey from Galilee to Jerusalem they have failed to understand his predictions about his death. Now in the passion narrative is their failure obvious. Watch out for the way in which Mark portrays them. In the garden of Gethsemane they all forsake him and flee. The last of them flees most shamefully, discarding his cloak as he races naked into the darkness and away from Jesus. Peter denies him. They are not present at Golgotha when Jesus dies. In fact, they are such a cowardly bunch that after Gethsemane Mark cannot bring himself to use the term "disciple" of them again.

Coming back for another look

Read the Gospel again later in the week and think about the following:

* Notice that Mark does not dwell on Jesus' physical pain. His treatment by the some of the Jewish authorities and by the Roman soldiers, while quite physical, is hardly torture. It is more akin to a mockery of Jesus as a false prophet and a false king. Mark does not describe the details of the crucifixion. Perhaps such details were too horrible to describe. But then Mark never shirks from telling it as it is. My own view is that, while not denying the terrible physical suffering of Jesus, Mark wants to emphasize Jesus' sense of loneliness and abandonment. Jesus has been betrayed by one of his friends, rejected by his own religious community, denied by another friend, condemned to death by the Roman state, mocked by passers-by, and even God is silent. No wonder he cries out "My God, my God, why have you abandoned me?"

The Season of Easter

The Season of Easter is the fifty-day period from Easter Sunday to Pentecost Sunday. It is the greatest liturgical season of the Church's year in which we celebrate Jesus' resurrection from the dead. The Greek word for Easter is *Páscha*, which is preserved in the Latin word *Pascha*. Both these words derive from the Hebrew word *Pesach*, meaning the Jewish festival of Passover, during which Jesus' death and resurrection occurred.

Many modern languages preserve the Latin word *Pascha* as *Pascua* (Italian), *Pasqua* (Spanish), *Páscoa* (Portuguese), and even as *Cáisc* (Irish). Our English word "Easter" developed from the Old English word *Ēostre*, which is the name of a pre-Christian Anglo-Saxon goddess who was worshipped during the month of April and whose cult involved rabbits and eggs!

The Christian understanding of Easter is connected directly with the Jewish festival of *Pesach*. This seven-day (or sometimes eight-day) festival commemorates the Exodus event, whereby the Israelites were freed by God from slavery in Egypt in the 13th century BC (Exodus 12:37–13:22). The date of Passover is determined by the Hebrew calendar, but it always falls on the night of the first full moon after the date of the northern hemisphere's vernal equinox (March 21st). Traditionally, Jewish people celebrate a special ritual meal called a *seder* on the first evening of the festival. According to the Synoptic Gospels, Jesus celebrated such a meal with his disciples on the Thursday night before he died. However, according to the Fourth Gospel, the Last Supper was not a formal Passover meal, but a farewell meal with Passover characteristics.

Easter is a moveable feast and the way in which its date is determined is complicated and contested between Western Christianity (Catholic and Protestant Churches) and Eastern Christianity (Orthodox Churches). Because of the close identity of the Last Supper with the Jewish Passover, the date of Easter has been determined in relation to the date of Passover. The First Council of Nicea (325 AD) decided the date of Easter as the first Sunday after the first full moon after the date of the March equinox. However, Western Christianity follows the Gregorian calendar, established by Pope Gregory XIII in 1582 AD, while Eastern Christianity follows the less astronomically accurate Julian calendar, established by Julius Caesar in 45 BC. Suffice to say that in Western Christianity Easter Sunday varies between March 22nd and April 25th while in Eastern Christianity it varies between April 4th and May 8th.

In 2012 Passover begins on the evening of Friday, April 6th, while Easter falls on Sunday, April 8th (Western Christianity) and on Sunday, April 15th (Eastern Christianity).

The liturgical colour for Easter is white. The Gospel texts for Eastertide are almost exclusively from John, with one text from Luke and one from Mark. It may surprise you that in the "Year of Mark" there is so little of his Gospel read on the Sundays of Easter. Mark's short account of the empty tomb (Mark 16:1-8) is read at the Easter Vigil this year. However, Mark's Gospel does not have many stories about the appearances of the Risen Lord. The stories that are in the Gospel are part of what is known as the *Longer Ending to Mark's Gospel*, which I will tell you about later. These are not stories original to the evangelist, but may have been borrowed from the Gospels of Matthew, Luke and John and subsequently added to Mark's Gospel.

So, on Easter Sunday, we read John's account of the visit to the empty tomb by Mary Magdalene, Peter and the other disciples and their gradual understanding of the teaching of the Resurrection. On the Second Sunday of Easter we read the Fourth Gospel's wonderful accounts of Jesus' appearances

to the disciples and how Thomas' disbelief gives way to faith. Luke offers the reading for the Third Sunday of Easter and offers another account of Jesus' appearance to the Jerusalem Community. The Fourth Sunday of Easter is traditionally known as "Good Shepherd Sunday" and we read Jesus' own description of himself as such in the Fourth Gospel. On the Fifth Sunday of Easter we read another text from the Fourth Gospel in which Jesus describes himself as the True Vine and his followers as the branches. We stay with the Fourth Gospel for the Sixth Sunday of Easter and read of Jesus' great command to love one another. For the solemnity of the Ascension of the Lord we read a short text from Mark. We complete Eastertide with a reading from the Fourth Gospel which tells of Jesus sending the Holy Spirit on his disciples.

Easter Sunday

8th April 2012

Preparing for Sunday
Read the Gospel: John 20:1-9

The explanation

According to the New Testament, God the Father raised Jesus from death to new life. The Church's faith in Jesus' resurrection is based primarily on his appearances to the disciples and not on the empty tomb. In fact, the empty tomb theme is one which emerges late in the development of the New Testament. The earliest statement of Easter faith comes from Paul (1 Corinthians 15:3-5) written about 53–54 AD. Paul says nothing about an empty tomb, but points to the appearances of the Risen Lord as the basis for Easter faith. The evangelists then took up the empty tomb theme some decades later, in the light of the Church's faith in the Resurrection based on Jesus' appearances. For the evangelists the empty tomb was the only explanation which would cover the conviction that Jesus was raised from the dead by the Father. Today we read John's account of the visit to the empty tomb by Mary Magdalene, Peter and the other disciples.

Mary Magdalene comes to the tomb early on Sunday morning before dawn. It is important to think of Mary as she is presented in the Gospels. She is not a sinful woman or a prostitute. These crude labels would develop in the centuries after the writing of the Gospels and would reach their height in the medieval period. According to the Fourth Gospel, she is the first to witness to the Resurrection and to proclaim the good news of Easter. On her arrival at the tomb she notes that the stone has been rolled away. Her interpretation of this is that someone has stolen Jesus' body. For this is what she reports to both Peter and the Beloved Disciple, having run to them. Her haste in running suggests urgency. Note that she says *"we* do not know ..." She is not just expressing her own puzzlement at the empty tomb, but also that of all Jesus' disciples.

Once Mary has made her report, the focus shifts to Peter and the Beloved Disciple. In the Fourth Gospel Peter is always presented as the leader and representative of the other disciples. The figure of the Beloved Disciple is more enigmatic. He is never named and always identified in his relationship with Jesus. His only role in the Gospel is to represent

body away. He has stolen away from death.

It is only now that the Beloved Disciple enters the tomb. The Gospel tells us that "he saw and believed." What did he believe? Is it Mary's report or is it faith in the Resurrection? What he believes in is the evidence of the empty tomb. He believes not simply that the tomb is empty, but that its emptiness bears witness to the Resurrection. These disciples have not yet met the Risen Lord and so scriptural faith in the Resurrection as such still awaits them. They will only come to full faith in Jesus' resurrection when they encounter the Risen Lord and he sends the Holy Spirit.

the love and intimacy with Jesus that characterize true discipleship.

These two disciples now set off for the empty tomb. Suddenly we learn that they break into a run to get there. It is a vivid detail that underscores haste and urgency. The Beloved Disciple wins the race and waits for Peter to catch up. But he does look into the tomb and sees the linen wrappings. Peter, always impulsive, has no hesitation and enters the tomb. He notes the linen wrappings and the place of the head cloth.

The evangelist has offered us a dramatic progression in what has been seen. Mary saw the stone rolled away. The Beloved Disciple saw the linen wrappings. Peter saw the wrappings and the head cloth. Mary's fear that the body was stolen is resolved. When stealing a body, grave robbers would never leave the burial garments behind. The implication is that no one has stolen Jesus'

Coming back for another look

Read the Gospel again later in the week and think about the following:

- It is worth spending some time this week thinking about the Beloved Disciple's faith. He saw an empty tomb and believed. In the account in the Fourth Gospel, there is no angelic messenger and no words of reassurance. So how can the Beloved Disciple come to faith? He believes because he has always trusted Jesus' words. When he sees the empty tomb, he knows what it means because of his absolute faith in Jesus.

Second Sunday of Easter

15 April 2012

Preparing for Sunday
Read the Gospel: John 20:19-31

The explanation

Jesus' first resurrection appearance to the disciples and then a week later to Thomas is told in today's reading from the Fourth Gospel. It is evening on the first Easter Sunday and the disciples are locked behind closed doors full of fear. The evangelist rarely refers to the Twelve (apostles) but more usually focuses on the whole community of Jesus' followers whom he calls "disciples." These clearly have not believed Mary Magdalene's report. They have shut themselves away "for fear of the Jews." Again it is important to understand this text in the context of John's community. The Fourth Gospel refers to the expulsion of Jewish Christians from the synagogue (John 9:22; 12:42; 16:2). There is much scholarly debate over whether such an event took place. Suffice to say that by the time the Fourth Gospel was written, the split between Judaism and Christianity was well underway, leaving Christians vulnerable to persecution by both the Jewish and Roman authorities. In today's Gospel the evangelist is telling his own community that Jesus' first followers also had to face frightening opposition from the Jewish authorities.

Jesus' greeting is one of peace. It is an ordinary greeting, still used in Israel today. Yet Jesus reminds this fear-filled group that, with his peace, there is no need to face the Jewish authorities with fear. Similarly John's own community will face the opposition of the Jewish authorities with the gift of Jesus' peace.

Jesus then shows the disciples his hands and side. The disciples break into rejoicing as the reality of his resurrection dawns on them. Notice how the evangelist makes his own confession of Easter faith by calling Jesus "Lord." Jesus repeats the greeting of peace. But this is not mere repetition. The disciples have finally come to recognize him as Risen Lord and the peace that only he can give. Jesus offers them peace and now sends them out to continue God's work. He breathes on them. The Bible often uses the verb "to breathe" when talking about God's acts of creation. Jesus' breathing the Holy Spirit on the disciples is, for the evangelist, a new act of creation. The Holy Spirit is the breath of the new life offered by God to all who believe in Jesus. It is this believing community, filled with the Holy Spirit, which will now continue God's work begun in Jesus.

Thomas is not present when Jesus appears to the disciples. When they tell Thomas the good news of the Resurrection, he does not believe. In fact, when they themselves had heard Mary Magdalene's report of meeting the Risen Lord, they didn't seem too eager to believe either. It took Jesus' appearance and the showing of his hands and side to them before they believed. So in asking to see and touch Jesus, Thomas is acting like the other disciples and is simply asking for the same proof they have been given. Jesus appears again a week later and, using Thomas' own words, offers him the proof he is looking for. Pay particular attention to how the last part of verse 27 is translated in the Sunday reading. The Greek text reads: "do not be unbelieving, but believing." There is nothing about "doubt" here and Thomas does not deserve the eternal moniker of "Doubter." Jesus is inviting Thomas to move from unbelief to belief, and offers himself, the Risen Lord, as the basis for this. Thomas' response to Jesus' offer is profound – "My Lord and my God!" Thomas recognizes, not only that Jesus is risen, but that he has ascended to the Father and shares God's glory. Thomas comes to this profound faith, not by touching Jesus, but by accepting Jesus' gift of himself. Jesus gives Thomas what he needs in order to believe.

Thomas and the other disciples have all come to faith because they have seen Jesus. Now Jesus offers a blessing to future believers, including you and me, who have come to faith without seeing.

Coming back for another look

Read the Gospel again later in the week and think about the following:

• The final verses of the reading (verses 30-31) bring the text to a close. Many biblical scholars believe that this was the original ending to the Gospel and that John 21 is a subsequent addition. Note carefully what the evangelist is saying in John 20:30-31. He is saying that you too can come to (a deeper) faith in Jesus, the Risen Lord.

Third Sunday of Easter

22nd April 2012

Preparing for Sunday
Read the Gospel: Luke 24:35-48

The explanation

Today's reading is from the Gospel of Luke and tells the story of Jesus' appearance to the Jerusalem community. It opens with the conclusion to Luke's previous story (Luke 24:13-35) about how two disciples met Jesus on the road as they travelled to a village called Emmaus, but did not recognize him. It was only when they were at table with him and he broke the bread that they recognized him as Risen Lord. They raced back to Jerusalem to tell the others and that's where we pick up today's story.

Luke's account of the appearance of the Risen Jesus has close parallels with the story in John 20:19-29 that we read last Sunday. These parallels are: Jesus' greeting of peace, his invitation to touch him, and the disciples' doubt. There is no evidence that one Gospel depends directly on the other. Rather, it may be that both Luke and John have independently developed a common tradition about Jesus' appearance to the disciples and used this tradition for their own theological purposes.

In Luke's story (as in John's) Jesus greets his disciples with the common greeting of "peace." Fear and doubt set in immediately. They are "startled and terrified." They doubt what they are experiencing and think it is a ghost. Yet they say nothing. The theme of doubting the experience of the Risen Jesus or of his resurrection is found also in the other three Gospels (Matthew 28:17; Mark 16:11.13-14; John 20:24-29). Jesus' response is first to question their doubting attitude and then to alleviate it by proving he is no ghost.

Jesus' first proof is to show them his hands and his feet. Luke is very clear that the Risen Lord has a living, physical body. Luke makes no mention of the nails or wounds of the crucifixion, as does John (John 20:25). Rather, Jesus' invitation to examine his hands and feet is to verify that his body is physically real. But this first proof doesn't work. The disciples still do not believe and remain in their wondering doubt. As is typical of Luke, he defends them and excuses their disbelief because of their joy! Jesus' second proof that he is physically alive is to eat some grilled fish in front of them. This is a proof he is not a ghost, but real. Curiously, Luke makes no comment on the effectiveness of this second proof. There is no report that the disciples believed in him. However, Luke wants to establish an important point. These disciples are eyewitnesses to the Resurrection and are those who ate and drank with him after he rose from the dead (Acts 10:41).

Jesus now gets the disciples both to look back in time and to look to the future. In looking back, he interprets the scriptures in relation to his death and resurrection. He reminds them of everything he had told them while he was with them. He had told them that he would die (Luke 9:22.44; 13:33; 17:25; 18:31-33). He had told them that everything in the scriptures about him would be fulfilled (Luke 18:31; 22:37). He refers to "the law of Moses, the prophets and the psalms." These are the three sections of the Hebrew scriptures with which Luke's readers would be familiar. In short, Jesus tells the disciples that everything in all of the scriptures has been fulfilled in his death and resurrection. Yet in order to get them to understand he opens their minds. The scriptures are not easily read and understood. A person's mind must be opened first in order to understand. Then the scriptures must be read in the light of his death and resurrection. Now Jesus adds one last idea. Not only are his death and resurrection the fulfilment of the scriptures, so too is the preaching of repentance to all nations in his name. The text ends with Jesus declaring that the disciples are witnesses. They are most suitable for this role because they can give

testimony to the suffering, death and resurrection of Jesus and proclaim the significance of Jesus with a living faith.

Coming back for another look

Read the Gospel again later in the week and think about the following:

• Our Easter faith rests on the scriptures and on the testimony of eyewitnesses who went to the tomb and who encountered Jesus as truly alive. The Church's proclamation of Easter faith is not based on fantasy or fiction. It is based on the experience of his first disciples who were his witnesses.

Fourth Sunday of Easter

29th April 2012

Preparing for Sunday
Read the Gospel: John 10:11-18

The explanation

Today is "Good Shepherd Sunday" and in the Gospel reading Jesus describes himself using the positive image of the "good shepherd" which he contrasts with the negative image of the "hired hand." The Greek word for "good" is *kalós*, but it also means "true" or "genuine." Jesus is claiming to be the "true" or "model" shepherd. But what kind of shepherd is he? He is one who is willing to die for his sheep.

In Jesus' day when shepherds finished their daily work they would round up the sheep and guide them into a sheep-pen. It was a rectangular stone structure about a metre high. But it had no gate. And when the sheep were all gathered in, the shepherd would lie across the open gate. If a wolf or a wild cat should attack the sheep or a thief should try to steal the sheep away, they would have to face the shepherd. Indeed, many a shepherd died while protecting his sheep. Unlike the "good shepherd" the "hired hand" is not willing to die for the sheep. He is only interested in the sheep for his own selfish purpose and for what he can get from

looking after them. So, when the sheep are threatened, he puts himself first and abandons the sheep to danger and destruction.

For a second time Jesus states that he is the "good shepherd." This time he uses the phrase based on the quality of his relationship with his followers and with God. He is a "good shepherd" because he "knows" his own who "know" him, just as he "knows" the Father and the Father "knows" him. Generally in the Bible, but specifically in the Fourth Gospel, inter-personal knowledge comes from mutual relationship. The degree to which one person knows another is based on the intimacy of their relationship. Similarly, one can only really know God if one has a close, personal, intimate relationship with God. The "good shepherd" has such a relationship not only with his sheep (his followers) but also with the Father. It is because of both these relationships that he lays down his life for his sheep and in doing so will bring unity to the flock.

In the final part of today's reading, Jesus leaves aside the shepherd image and focuses on his own death and his relationship with the Father. In these short verses the evangelist identifies three theological themes which are essential for understanding the death of Jesus in the Fourth Gospel. The first is that Jesus lays down his life out of love. The evangelist has already told us that God loves the world (John 3:16) and Jesus (John 3:35). Now we learn that God loves Jesus because of his willingness to lay down his life for his followers. Jesus not only commands his followers to love one another, he does so too. He models what that love is like through his obedience to the Father and by his willingness to lay down his life. In short, Jesus' death is the ultimate expression of his love for God and for the world.

The second theme is that Jesus lays down his life freely and in obedience to God. He is not anyone's victim, but remains in control of his life to its end. The final theme is that Jesus' death and resurrection are connected. He lays down his (earthly) life in order to take up his (risen) life. This is unique to the Fourth Gospel. Generally in the New Testament it is God (the Father) who raises Jesus from death. Here Jesus takes

up his life by the power given him by the Father.

Coming back for another look

Read the Gospel again later in the week and think about the following:

- Jesus is the Good Shepherd who knows you. He knows you by name. He has a relationship with you unlike any other.

In our modern culture and in the electronic age, this is something crucially important. We have all been reduced to numbers by our electronic so-called knowledge-based economy: driver's licence numbers, credit card numbers, PIN numbers for this and for that. We are coded and numbered and locked into computers all over the place. Jesus will have none of this. We matter to him. All people matter to him because we belong to him and he belongs to us. He is the God who knows us all intimately and calls us by name.

Fifth Sunday of Easter

6 May 2012

Preparing for Sunday
Read the Gospel: John 15:1-8

The explanation

In last Sunday's Gospel Jesus proclaimed, "I am the good shepherd." Today's Gospel contains another "I Am" saying – "I am the true vine." This text is not easy to understand. It's quite dense in places and uses a lot of wordplay based on the original Greek that is lost in translation. Still, let me offer my explanation. Not only does Jesus draw on an image that was common throughout the Mediterranean, but it is also a key image in the Jewish scriptures. The Bible often presents Israel as a vine and God as the planter or vinedresser. However, when Jesus uses this image he is saying something about himself (the vine) in relationship with the Father (the vinedresser) and in relationship with his followers (the branches). Only when the vinedresser, the vine and the branches are in a harmonious relationship is fruit produced. If Jesus is the vine, then his Father is clearly the vinedresser, for it is God who energizes and directs Jesus and his work. Jesus describes himself as a vine that is "true" or "authentic." He is such a vine because he comes from the Father and is in relationship with the Father.

God, the vinedresser, removes (in Greek "cuts off") fruitless branches from the vine, but prunes (in Greek "cuts clean") fruitful ones so they can bear even more fruit. Again the image would be easily understood by a Mediterranean audience. But what is the "fruit" that Jesus speaks of? It is the love that members of the Christian community must have for one another. The fruitless branches are those within the Christian community who fail to love, while the fruitful branches are those who imitate Jesus' love. The disciples have already been pruned. In Greek, the verb "to cleanse" also means "to prune." The disciples have been cleansed or pruned by Jesus' own words to them and by "abiding" in relationship with him. Just as the branches "abide" on the vine, so the disciples "abide" in Jesus.

Jesus develops further this idea of abiding in him by using another agricultural image. Vine branches that stay connected to the vine thrive and bear grapes. Those that are disconnected, wither, dry up, bear no fruit and end up in the vinedresser's fire. It is vivid language, which Jesus uses to make a dramatic point about choice. We can choose to be in relationship with Jesus (the branches connected to the vine) or we can choose to reject such a relationship (the fruitless, withered branches). The choice and its consequences are ours.

The final part of today's text takes up ideas that are found elsewhere in the Fourth Gospel. If Jesus' followers abide in him and let his words abide in them, their prayers will be answered (John 14:13-14). If they continue both to bear the fruit of love and to be his disciples then they will continue his work and God will be glorified through them (John 14:12). Today's reading ends half-way through this demanding discourse, but we will read the remainder of it next Sunday.

Coming back for another look

Read the Gospel again later in the week and think about the following:

• This text is a demanding one, not just in terms of its interpretation, but also in terms of the model of faith community or Church it reveals. Jesus presents a model in which all his followers are equal, are connected in relationship to him, and glorify God by bearing the fruit of his love to the world. The writer of the Fourth Gospel does not envisage the hierarchical Church found elsewhere in the New Testament. The model offered here is one based on a radical equality. All members of the Church are equal and are co-responsible for one another and to one another. I cannot help but think that it is urgent for all in the Church, but most especially for those in leadership, to contemplate Jesus' words. I'm sure that the abuse crisis would have unfolded differently if Church leaders had listened not just to legal and psychological experts but to the co-equal "branches" that are the victims and their parents. If our leaders had done so, our Church would not be in its current scandalous mess. Will Church leaders start now to listen to the ordinary faithful – not just on the abuse scandals but on the wide range of critical issues that are affecting Church life? I can only hope.

Sixth Sunday of Easter

13th May 2012

Preparing for Sunday
Read the Gospel: John 15:9-17

The explanation

Today's reading continues from where we left off last Sunday. You will recall how Jesus called himself the "true vine" and his disciples the "branches." That text ended with Jesus talking about his disciples "abiding "in him or being connected to him. Today's text picks up on that idea and develops it. As with last Sunday's text, it is not easy to understand. For Jesus, the only way in which the disciples can "abide" in him or be in relationship with him is by living out the love that he and the Father share. If they can live out that love, then they can also share in Jesus' joy. Jesus sets out what he means by such love. It is to love others in the way that Jesus has loved the disciples. Pay particular attention to verse 13. This is the clearest statement in the Gospel about loving as Jesus does. Greek ideas about friendship understood death for one's friends as a noble ideal. Jesus has already hinted that his death for his disciples is the sign of his love. He implied this when he called himself the "good shepherd" who lays down his life (John 10:17-18) and when he washed their feet (John 13:1-15). The Greek word for "friend" (*phílos*) and the verb "to love" (*philéō*) are connected in meaning. When Jesus calls his disciples "friends," he is saying that he loves them. In simple terms, to be Jesus' friend is to be loved by him and to love him.

When he washed their feet he used the language of master and servant (John 13:1-15). That language is now transformed – he calls his disciples "friends." They are his friends because he has told them everything about God. He has kept nothing back. Not only that, but he has invited them to join in the intimacy of his relationship with the Father. The language of friendship is now suddenly replaced by the language of choice or, as theologians sometimes call it, "election." It is Jesus who has chosen or elected the disciples. It is Jesus who has chosen or elected you and me. Jesus' choice of the disciples is one whereby he sends them out to bear lasting fruit by loving as he does. Today's text ends with Jesus, once again, commanding his followers to love one another according to his way of loving.

For the last three Sundays we have been reading some long and difficult texts from the Fourth Gospel. In these readings Jesus gives a speech or discourse calling himself the "good shepherd" and the "true vine." He commands his disciples to love one another as he has loved them – with a love generous to the point of dying for one another.

These speeches come from a section of the Fourth Gospel known as the Last Supper Discourse (John 13–17). It is a section of the Gospel in which Jesus gives his "last will and testament" to the disciples. As Risen and Ascended Lord, he leaves them. Yet in doing so, he offers them guidance on how they are to live and to love, faithful to him in the years after the Resurrection.

Coming back for another look

Read the Gospel again later in the week and think about the following:

•   There are many reasons why Eastertide is such a joyful season. During this time it is important to remember the various gifts Jesus has bequeathed you in his last will and testament. Not only has he given you his guidance on how to be a faithful disciple, he has also gifted you with his peace and bestowed God's Holy Spirit on you.

There is one other gift I would like you to recall as you read this text. Jesus has given you the incredible gift of his friendship. You are his friend because he chose you and he loves you. This is a gift he will never take back, no matter what happens in your life. This might be a good time to think about what it means for you to have Jesus as a friend. It might also be a suitable time to think about what it means for Jesus to have a friend like you.

The feast of the Ascension

20 May 2012

Preparing for Sunday
Read the Gospel: Mark 16:15-20

The explanation

Today we celebrate the Ascension of the Lord. We believe that Jesus, our Risen Lord, was taken bodily into the presence of the Father. We profess this belief every Sunday when we recite the Creed. There are many New Testament references to the Ascension. Three of the four Gospels refer to Jesus' return to the Father (Mark 16:19; Luke 24:50-53 and John 20:17.22). Luke also refers to the Ascension in Acts 1:3. As you have already seen, the writer of the Fourth Gospel understands that Jesus' death, resurrection and ascension all took place in a single moment.

It is Luke, writing in Acts, who suggests that Jesus' Ascension took place forty days after his Resurrection and ten days before Pentecost. Traditionally, the Church has followed Luke's pattern and celebrated the Ascension forty days after Easter, on Ascension Thursday. Since 1996 the Irish Church has celebrated the feast on the Seventh Sunday of Easter. The Church in England and Wales followed suit in 2007, while the Church in Scotland retains the traditional Ascension Thursday.

Today's reading is taken from Mark 16, which is a hugely problematic final chapter to his Gospel. Biblical scholarship is in wide agreement that Mark the Evangelist finished his Gospel at Mark 16:8. It is a stark ending to a sombre Gospel. The women who discover the empty tomb and who receive the good news of Jesus' Resurrection flee from the scene terrified. They return home and are silenced by fear. This ending is consistent with Mark's view that fear destroys discipleship, even when confronted with the good news of the Resurrection.

Since the Gospel ends so abruptly and harshly, an unknown writer (150 AD?) attempted to bring it to a gentler conclusion. So the Gospel has three possible endings. There is Mark's at Mark 16:8. Then there is the Shorter Ending, which is usually found between Mark 16:8 and Mark 16:9 but does not have a verse number and, finally, the Longer Ending to Mark's Gospel (Mark 16:9-20). The Longer Ending seems to consist of resurrection appearances borrowed from the other three Gospels (Matthew 28:18-20; Luke 8:2; 24:13-53 and John 20:19-29). Yet it would be wrong to suggest that the writer of the Longer Ending is simply recycling other Gospel stories. First, the writer wants to overcome the apparent shame of the women's flight and fear-induced scandal and wants to highlight Jesus' command to spread the Gospel.

The writer is well-intentioned, but has betrayed Mark the Evangelist somewhat. Mark's intended ending leaves you to struggle with the women's fear-induced silence. The writer of the Longer Ending has short-circuited your engagement with their silence and fear by giving you the ending that Christians wanted in the second century AD.

Today's reading is taken from Mark 16:15-20, which deals with Jesus commissioning the disciples and the account of his Ascension. In this the writer is following closely the Gospel of Luke. However, the writer goes well beyond Luke. For the writer of the Longer Ending offers a portrait of Jesus, the Son of God, the Suffering Servant, and God's Messiah enthroned in heaven at the right hand of God. Jesus' heavenly triumph is accompanied by an earthly one – the successful worldwide proclamation of the Gospel.

Coming back for another look

Read the Gospel again later in the week and think about the following:

• We read the Longer Ending to Mark's Gospel because it contains a reference to the

Ascension. The primary reason for the Longer Ending is the abrupt ending at Mark 16:8 with its focus on the women's flight and fright. It's a stark reminder that the followers of Jesus (then and now) are not superheroes. That which pinned Jesus to the cross can all too easily reduce his followers to fearful silence and flight. Yet the Gospel of Mark is a Gospel for hard times. Even when we experience our own weakness, the fragility of our faith and the helplessness of our world, Mark's Gospel is a reminder that God can draw out our courageous faith and empower us. Jesus, our Risen Lord, has not abandoned us and never will.

The Feast of Pentecost

27th May 2012

Preparing for Sunday
Read the Gospel: John 20:19-23

The explanation

The word "Pentecost" comes from the Greek phrase *Pentēkostē (hēmera)*, which means "the fiftieth (day)" and refers to the great feast which is celebrated fifty days after Easter Sunday. Today we recall the descent of the Holy Spirit on the first disciples and the birth of the Christian Church.

We have already seen that the Jewish feast of Passover and the Christian feast of Easter have certain parallels. Something similar occurs with the Christian feast of Pentecost and the Jewish feast of Shavuot or Weeks (which is celebrated in May or June). Shavuot falls fifty days after the Passover. Passover celebrates God's deliverance of Israel from slavery, while Shavuot celebrates God's gift of the Torah (Jewish scriptures) and the birth of Israel as God's People.

Pentecost falls fifty days after Easter Sunday. Easter celebrates God's deliverance of humanity from death through Jesus' resurrection, while Pentecost celebrates God's gift of the Holy Spirit and the birth of the New Israel that is the Church.

You have already studied today's reading (John 20:19-23) as part of the text for the Second Sunday of Easter (John 20:19-31). It would be good to turn back now to pages 74-75 and re-read the explanation given for that Sunday.

Coming back for another look

Read the Gospel again later in the week and think about the following:

- Remember that for the writer of the Fourth Gospel Jesus' death, resurrection and ascension all occur in a single moment on Golgotha. Now as Risen and Ascended Lord he gifts his disciples with the Holy Spirit and commissions them to do God's work. What exactly are they to do? They are to love one another and in doing so reveal God to the world. It is by revealing God that they will make it possible for people to enter into an intimate relationship with God. If people choose a close relationship with God, their sins will be forgiven; if they reject such a relationship, their sins will remain.

The writer of the Fourth Gospel has a clear understanding of what Jesus is asking of his Church – to offer unending witness to God's love made visible in Jesus.

Peace be with you!

As the Father has sent me, I am sending you

And with that he breathed on them and said,

Receive the Holy Spirit

Jesus came and stood among them and said, "Peace be with you!

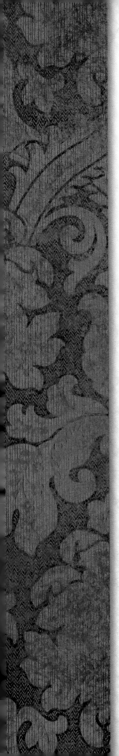

Ordinary Time II

Ordinary Time II resumes on Monday, May 28th and continues until Saturday, December 1st. The week when Ordinary Time resumes is determined by the date of Easter and the fact that there are only 34 weeks in Ordinary Time. In 2012 Ordinary Time resumes in its Eighth Week on Monday, May 28th. But we do not resume the regular celebration of the Sundays in Ordinary Time until the Thirteenth Sunday (July 1st) as three major solemnities intervene. These are: Trinity Sunday (June 3rd), the Solemnity of the Most Holy Body and Blood of Christ (June 10th), and the Solemnity of the Nativity of John the Baptizer (June 24th). During the remaining 22 weeks of Ordinary Time the Sunday Gospel readings are taken largely from the Gospel of Mark. However, some readings are also taken from the Gospels of Matthew, Luke and John. We do not begin to read Mark's Gospel in a consistent manner until the Thirteenth Sunday in Ordinary Time. The effect of all this is that there is a section of Mark's Gospel which we will not get to read in 2012. I would like to summarize briefly that part of Mark' Gospel so you can resume reading it consistently from July 1st. You will need to read these texts for yourself using your Bible.

Jesus gets into a controversy over fasting (Mark 2:18-22), which was very much part of Jewish traditional practice in the first century AD. Jesus does not seem to have practiced fasting with great regularity. In fact, the distinctive mark of his ministry was table fellowship. He liked to eat and drink with all kinds of people. In doing so he shared his life with them. The Pharisees were very strict about who they ate with. Not only did they wish to avoid sinners, they were also concerned that any food served at table was kosher or prepared according to the strictest dietary laws of the Bible. Jesus simply did not share these concerns. He saw fasting as an inappropriate way for celebrating the approach of the Kingdom of God. But he did envisage a time when fasting would be appropriate – a time when the bridegroom would be "taken away." In other words, only after Jesus' death would fasting be appropriate for his disciples.

A further controversy follows immediately (Mark 2:23–3:6). It is triggered when Jesus' disciples were passing through a cornfield and picked the heads of grain. They were on pilgrimage. They had been walking for a long time and were hungry. The ears of corn were inviting and so they ate. But it was the Sabbath and they broke the Jewish law. So Jesus gets into a controversial debate with the Pharisees about the law of the Sabbath. For Jesus, the needs of the hungry always take priority over rules and regulations, and if the Sabbath could not be celebrated in such a spirit, then it was better not to celebrate it at all. Later on that same Sabbath day in the local synagogue, as if to prove his point, he healed a man with a withered hand. This was the last straw for the Pharisees and the supporters of the King of Galilee, Herod Antipas. They began to conspire together in order to destroy him.

Mark now takes up the theme of Jesus and his "new family" of disciples (Mark 3:20-35). The story begins with the amazing admission that Jesus' own blood relatives come and try to stop him in his ministry because they are convinced he is insane. They simply do not understand his urgent preaching about the Kingdom. If they think he is insane, the Jewish scribes argue that he is possessed. He rejects this with a stinging counter argument. How could Satan be behind his own defeat? Jesus' new family does not consist of those who are connected to him by blood (his relatives) or by Jewish tradition (the scribes). Rather, the members of his new family are those who do the will of God. Mark challenges his readers to be members of Jesus' family by doing God's will.

Jesus' parables are all found in Mark 4. The Gospel reading for the Eleventh Sunday in Ordinary Time (Mark 4:26-34) deals with two of these parables and I will give you their explanation below. Finally, Jesus calms a storm on the Sea of Galilee (Mark 4:35-41). It is a story that once again raises the question about Jesus' identity and invites us to trust him in the midst of life's storms.

Trinity Sunday

3rd June 2012

Preparing for Sunday

Read the Gospel: Matthew 28:16-20

The explanation

The first Sunday after Pentecost has always been known as Trinity Sunday. The liturgical colour for the feast is white. On this day the Church celebrates that which is the essence of the Christian faith and which sets Christianity apart from all other religions, namely our belief in the Most Holy Trinity. I am not going to attempt to explain the doctrine of the Trinity. If I could, it would take this entire book to begin to do so! We Christians believe that God is a unity of three divine persons (Father, Son and Holy Spirit) and that God the Son and God the Holy Spirit have exactly the same nature as God the Father. At its most basic, this doctrine asserts the essentially complex and mysterious nature of God. The New Testament does not use the term "Trinity" or attempt to offer any Trinitarian teaching. The doctrine about the Trinity evolved over centuries after the New Testament was written. However, the New Testament offered texts which helped to formulate our belief in the Trinity. One such text is

the Gospel for today's Eucharist.

This text from Matthew's Gospel is also known as "The Great Commission," because in it Jesus commissions his disciples to preach the Gospel to the world. The eleven disciples have gathered together for the first time following Jesus' arrest, trial and crucifixion. Their number has been reduced from twelve by Judas' suicide (Matthew 27:3-10). While Matthew does not say it explicitly, we presume that they have received the message from the women who found the empty tomb (Matthew 28:1-7) and, in obedience to the angel's message, have gone to Galilee.

Jesus appears to them. They see him and worship him, though there is doubt. The Greek text leaves open a number of possibilities. It could be read that "some apart from the eleven doubted." Or it could be read as "some of the eleven doubted." It could even be read as "(all) those who worshipped him doubted." What is not in doubt is that the faith of these disciples wavered with doubt! Even in the presence of the Risen Lord, their faith was not perfect. Matthew does not offer any teaching on the divine nature of Jesus. This would be worked

The Year of the Suffering Servant

out in the centuries after Matthew's Gospel. Yet, for Matthew, to encounter Jesus is to encounter God.

Jesus speaks to his disciples. He, the Risen Lord, is Lord of heaven and earth. He speaks with God's authority and there is no blasphemy in worshipping him. He sends them as his disciples to all the nations of the world. Pay particular attention to verse 19 – for this is one of the key texts for the future development of the doctrine of the Trinity. Matthew has no developed doctrine of the Trinity. He does mention the "Father, Son and Holy Spirit" but does not explain how they might relate to each other. Matthew and the other New Testament writers are utterly convinced of the unity of God as expressed in Judaism. Yet when they talk about the One God, they use the threefold pattern of Father, Son and Holy Spirit, which will eventually become the doctrine of the Trinity.

Notice also the last words of Jesus in this Gospel – "I am with you always..." At the beginning of the Gospel we read that Jesus was the Emmanuel foretold by the prophet Isaiah (Isaiah 7:14). The Hebrew name Emmanuel means "God-is-with-us." With the birth of Jesus, God promised to be with us always. At the end of the Gospel, as Risen Lord, Jesus promises once again to be Emmanuel. This was a message that comforted Christians through many of the crises they would face throughout history and must surely comfort us in these scandal-ridden times for our Church.

Coming back for another look

Read the Gospel again later in the week and think about the following:

- Today Jesus is continually present in his disciples. It is to us, his worshipping and wavering Church, that he has given the mission to proclaim the Gospel to the world. Our discipleship is characterized by both faith and doubt. I am convinced that doubt is essential for genuine adult faith, because doubt keeps the mind and heart open to truth, no matter how difficult or mysterious. If we are prepared to face our doubts honestly and pursue the truth relentlessly, then our faith can only become stronger.

The Most Holy Body and Blood of Christ

10th June 2012

Preparing for Sunday
Read the Gospel: Mark 14:12-16.22-26

The explanation

Today's feast does not commemorate any particular event in Jesus' life, but is a celebration of his gift of the Eucharist. The traditional day for this celebration is the Thursday after Trinity Sunday. The reason Thursday is chosen is because Jesus celebrated the Last Supper on the Thursday before he died when, according to the Synoptic Gospels, he gifted his disciples with the Eucharist during the Passover meal. Many local Churches have moved the celebration to the Sunday after Trinity Sunday. The Churches in Ireland and in the UK follow this practice. The liturgical colour for the feast is white.

The Gospel text is from Mark's Gospel. As you have already seen, Mark understands that the Last Supper was a Passover meal. So it is that the disciples ask him naturally about his plans to celebrate the Passover and about his instructions to prepare for the meal. Jesus sends two of them into the city and tells them what they are to do.

In this way Mark shows that Jesus knows what is about to happen to him and engages in the whole process in a deliberate and calm manner. Normally, the Passover meal would be celebrated by a Jewish family. However, Jesus is not going to celebrate this meal with blood relatives but with his "new family" of disciples. When the disciples go into the city, everything happens as Jesus foretold and they make the preparations.

Later that evening, during the Passover meal, Jesus speaks words about his death over the bread and wine. Following the Jewish custom at Passover, Jesus blesses God for the gift of food and then breaks the bread into pieces and gives a piece to all present with the words, "Take, this is my body." The broken bread he shares with the disciples is his body broken in death for others. Those who eat this bread are now connected to him in the most profound way.

He does the same with the cup and adds, "This is my blood of the covenant, which is poured out for many." Judaism understood that the covenant made between God and Israel at Mount Sinai had been sealed in animals' blood (Exodus 24:4-8). Blood symbolized life and since the Sinai Covenant was sealed in blood, it meant that Israel then shared in God's life. Jesus now offers an eternal life-giving New Covenant, sealed in his own blood, which is poured out "for many." This phrase is a Hebrew idea and does not mean that Jesus' blood was shed just for some people as opposed to all people. The Hebrew idea is that the action of one person (Jesus) will benefit many others (more than one person). However, the number of these others is infinite. This is an important point as Mark's phrasing is now used in the new English translation of the Eucharistic Prayer, where it should not be interpreted as limiting Jesus' saving action to a restricted number of people.

Finally, Jesus talks about that day when he will drink wine in the heavenly banquet. In recalling these words, Mark reminds us that Jesus' death is not the end of this story. Jesus predicts his resurrection and the fullness of God's Kingdom which will be brought about by his death. Jewish Passover meals usually ended with the joyful singing of Psalms 114–118, and Mark tells us that the Last Supper ends with this Passover ritual.

Coming back for another look

Read the Gospel again later in the week and think about the following:

• While Mark's Gospel is the oldest, it does not contain the earliest New Testament tradition about the Last Supper. We have to turn to Paul (1 Corinthians 11: 23-25) for that tradition (55 AD) which predates Mark's (70 AD) by about 15 years. Both Paul and Mark tell us that at the Last Supper Jesus took bread and wine and spoke his words over them. Paul also tells us that Jesus added, "Do this ... in remembrance of me."

In commanding us to do the same as he did, he was saying to us "take your body and give it for others and break it for others in love. Take the cup of your blood and pour it out and empty it and hold it out so that others may be whole again." The first disciples probably did not fully understand what he did that Thursday night. It gradually dawned on them that Jesus would repeat this giving of himself, time and time again, in us.

Eleventh Sunday in Ordinary Time

17th June 2012

Preparing for Sunday
Read the Gospel: Mark 4:26-34

The explanation

Today we return briefly to Ordinary Time and the Gospel of Mark. We pick up the story as Jesus is still ministering in Galilee. One of the features of Jesus' ministry was his use of parables. Mark's Gospel contains some parables, which, apart from the Parable of the Wicked Tenants (Mark 12:1-12), are all found in Mark 4. These have to do with seeds, their mysterious growth, and the Kingdom of God.

Seeds are mysterious. Their genetic code for a new generation of life is contained in a tiny, hard and dry piece of matter. We can create the right environment for a seed to grow but we cannot make it grow. If seeds are mysterious to us, imagine how far more so to Galilean farmers in the first century AD. Their hope for the future depended on the sprouting of seeds. A drought could wipe out a whole season's work, and bring about famine. On the other hand, rain at the right time and favourable growing conditions would mean the difference between life and death, between plenty and hunger. The seed was not just an abstract image of life – it was life itself. The seed-parables we read today are the Parable of the Seed Growing Secretly (Mark 4:26-29) and the Parable of the Mustard Seed (Mark 4:30-32).

The Parable of the Seed Growing Secretly is found only in Mark. It stresses the mysterious growth of the seed that is beyond human control. The harvest comes about in three stages. First, the seed is sown. Then, while the farmer goes about his normal routine of life, the seed grows and "he does not know" how. Finally, only when the grain is ripe does the farmer come into play again when his skill is called for. The point of the parable is that once the seed is sown, the farmer lets it be and trusts the soil to bring about growth, even though he does not understand the process. When the grain is ripe, then he knows that he must act to gather in the harvest. Jesus has sown the seeds of his word. Now, in this present time, those seeds are growing, even though we cannot see anything dramatic happening. We cannot speed up or slow down the coming of the Kingdom. However, its plentiful harvest will take place if we but trust God.

The Parable of the Mustard Seed, which is also found in the other Synoptic Gospels (Matthew 13:31-32 and Luke 13:18-19), deals with the apparent insignificance of the Kingdom of God in the present time. It stresses again the amazing contrast between the tiny seed and the vast outcome resulting from its growth. The small seed turns into a great tree in which the birds of heaven build their nests. Jesus is using exaggerated speech here. The mustard seed is not the smallest of seeds but was thought of as such proverbially. It does not grow into a great tree, but only into shrub two or three metres high. Jesus' original audience knew well that mustard shrubs could grow quite vigorously and take over an entire garden sooner or later. Small birds could indeed find shade in their branches. The message of the parable is that all kinds of faithful people will find a home in the Kingdom and God will protect them. However, they should not be disheartened by the Kingdom's humble beginnings.

The message of these two seed parables is clear. The Kingdom of God is a mysterious thing. Its beginnings may be modest or even insignificant like the mustard seed. It will grow, but its growth does not depend on human action. Like the farmer, God scatters the mysterious seed of the Kingdom through Jesus, hoping that it will take root and produce a harvest.

Coming back for another look

Read the Gospel again later in the week and think about the following:

*   Mark reminds us at the end of the reading that Jesus always chose to speak to people in parables. The crowds do not really understand the parables because they are not able to listen to him fully. His parables seem like riddles to most people. Even his own disciples cannot understand them. So he explains the parables in private to these disciples who are now his "new family." Yet even still they do not fully understand Jesus. They will have to journey with him to Jerusalem, to Golgotha and to the empty tomb, before they finally can understand him.

The Nativity of John the Baptizer

24th June 2012

Preparing for Sunday

Read the Gospel: Luke 1:57-66.80

The explanation

We have already met John the Baptizer on the Second and Third Sundays of Advent (pages 12-15 above). You might like to go back and re-read these sections. Today we celebrate John's birth and the Gospel text is taken from Luke. According to Luke's account, John's parents were Zechariah and Elizabeth, who are of priestly decent. However, they are both old and Elizabeth is barren (Luke 1:5-7). One day when Zechariah is serving in the Temple, he receives a visitation from the angel Gabriel (whose name means the Power of God). Gabriel has wonderful news for Zechariah. By the power of God he is going to have a son, whom he must name John. Naturally enough, Zechariah is not too sure about this and expresses his doubt. Gabriel assures him that it will be so, but because of his doubt he will be struck mute until these events actually happen (Luke 1:8-23). Zechariah heads home and Elizabeth conceives (Luke 1:24-25). Later on we learn that when the angel Gabriel announces to Mary that she is to be the mother of Jesus, Elizabeth is already six months pregnant (Luke 1:36). Since the Church celebrates Jesus' birth on December 25th, John's birth is celebrated six months previously on June 24th. The liturgical colour for the feast is white.

Today's text tells the story of John's birth. Luke's account of the actual birth is brief. Yet when Elizabeth's neighbours hear about it they react by saying that "the Lord had shown his great mercy to her." This is typical of Luke, for whom the focus is always God's merciful love.

As a Jewish male baby, John is circumcised eight days after his birth according to the Jewish law. It is during this ritual that a Jewish baby boy receives his name. Everyone expects that he will be called Zechariah after his dad. Yet, suddenly and dramatically, Elizabeth declares that he is to be named John. This is the name the angel had given to Zechariah in the Temple (Luke 1:13), and since Zechariah had been struck mute, Luke suggests that Elizabeth decided on the name in some miraculous and independent way. This causes confusion among the guests and they consult Zechariah. They make gestures to him. Zechariah responds by writing

The Year of the Suffering Servant

and declares that the child's name will be John. Everything that Gabriel had told Zechariah has come to pass.

Suddenly Zechariah can hear and speak again and he breaks into praise of God. His lengthy hymn of praise, known as the Benedictus (Luke 1:67-79), is not read in today's Gospel. You might like to read it for yourself, as it is a wonderful prayer in praise of God's mercy and love. All these dramatic events incite fear and amazement among the assembled guests and they begin to speculate about the child's future. Yet Zechariah knows what John is going to be because Gabriel has already told him (Luke 1:15-17). Read these verses for yourself.

The final verse of today's reading bridges the gap between John's birth and his ministry (Luke 1:80). He grows up right in front of us and is ready to begin his work of preparing the way for the Messiah.

Coming back for another look

Read the Gospel again later in the week and think about the following:

* All four Gospels tell of John's baptism and preaching at the River Jordan. It is there that he acknowledges Jesus as the Messiah and baptizes him. You have already read Mark's account of this on the feast of the Baptism of the Lord (pages 30-31 above). You might like to re-read that section at this point. John eventually gathers a group of disciples who, according to the Acts of the Apostles, gradually join Jesus' followers (Acts 18:24-19:6).

John dies a martyr's death (Matthew 14:3-12 and Mark 6:17-29) at the command of the king of Galilee, Herod Antipas, whose adulterous lifestyle John had publicly denounced. The Jewish historian Flavius Josephus (37–100? AD) suggests in his *Antiquities of the Jews* that Herod had John arrested and executed because John had so many followers that Herod feared they might begin a rebellion. Both the religious and political reasons are probably true. In any case, John lived and died a courageous witness to Jesus the Messiah.

Thirteenth Sunday in Ordinary Time

1st July 2012

Preparing for Sunday
Read the Gospel: Mark 5:21-43

The explanation

Mark likes to use a technique that allows him to tell two stories at the same time. He takes a story, divides it into two parts, then inserts a second story between the two parts of the first story. In today's reading, the story of The Woman with a Haemorrhage (Mark 5:25-34) is inserted into the story of The Raising of Jairus' Daughter (Mark 5:21-24.35-43). This technique is sometimes known as a "Markan sandwich" and it is not always easy to interpret. For the purposes of the explanation, I will separate out the two stories.

Jesus has just crossed the Sea of Galilee and is about to teach the people gathered there when a synagogue official called Jairus begs him to come and heal his sick daughter. It's an unusual request from someone of the religious establishment which has shown itself resistant to Jesus and his message. But Jairus is also a parent and he is desperate. Jesus agrees to heal the child and heads for Jairus' house followed by a crowd. It is while he is on his way that he engages with a woman with a haemorrhage, whom he heals.

If this delay causes Jairus any anxiety, Mark doesn't report it. Suddenly the situation becomes tragic. Messengers arrive. The little girl is dead. There is no point in bothering Jesus any further. Jesus overhears the message and invites Jairus to stay on the journey of faith. In the Greek text Jesus tells him: "Do not fear; just keep on believing."

When Jesus gets to the house, the only disciples he allows enter are Peter, James and John. They seem to be part of his inner circle. They will see his glory at the Transfiguration (Mark 9:2-9) and his anguish in Gethsemane (Mark 14:32-42). There is also a large crowd of friends and relatives gathered in shock and mourning, who meet Jesus' statement that the girl is not dead with derisive laughter.

So Jesus sends them out for there is no place for unbelief in what he is about to do. He invites the little girl's parents to join him, together with the three disciples. Taking the child by the hand he says in Aramaic (his native tongue), Talitha qum! which Mark translates as "little girl, arise!" It is one of the few places where Jesus' words spoken in his own tongue have been preserved. Mark also says that the child was twelve years old. She has had life for as long as the other woman has had haemorrhages. Like the older woman, the little girl has been given life and a future by Jesus.

The cure of the woman with the haemorrhage takes place while Jesus was on his way to Jairus' house. This woman is suffering unbelievably. She has been bleeding for twelve years. She has gone from doctor to doctor, spending all her money on one useless treatment after another. She is broke and she is getting worse. In Jesus' day, blood was considered to be a person's life-force. People who bled were avoided and isolated out of fear of (ritual) contamination. So along with the haemorrhaging, the woman was socially isolated and marginalized within her own community. She had no life and no future. She has heard about Jesus and, summoning up her faith, she touches his clothes. She is cured instantly. The years of suffering are over and she has a life and a future again. Yet Jesus, aware that power has gone out from him, wants to meet her. His miracles are not anonymous, magic events. They are personal encounters in faith. When she comes forward and tells her story, it is her way of proclaiming who Jesus is and what he has done for her.

Coming back for another look

Read the Gospel again later in the week and think about the following:

- Jesus' power to heal can overcome all barriers that isolate and imprison us. Jairus was isolated by being part of the religious establishment that could never been seen to recognize Jesus or his power. Yet his love for his daughter triggered within him the courage and faith to cross that barrier and save his daughter. The woman was isolated by her haemorrhagic illness. Yet her desperation for a life in the community led her to touch Jesus in faith. Both were freed.

What are the barriers to freedom in your life? What might it mean for you to hear Jesus say to you today: "Do not fear; just keep on believing"?

Fourteenth Sunday in Ordinary Time

8th July 2012

Preparing for Sunday
Read the Gospel: Mark 6:1-6a

The explanation

Last Sunday we read how Jesus performed two miracles based on faith. He raised Jairus' daughter from the dead and healed a woman with a haemorrhagic illness. Both Jairus and the woman believed in him and so he could work life-enhancing miracles for them. Today's reading deals with a visit by Jesus to his hometown of Nazareth with his new family of disciples. Much has happened since he last was in Nazareth. He has demonstrated his authority over demons, illness and death. Many have come to faith in him, especially in Capernaum where he now lives. However, it was in Nazareth that his own natural family had believed he was insane and had tried to stop his mission (Mark 3:21). Has anything changed? Will they and the other Nazarenes now believe in him?

As is his practice he goes to the synagogue to preach. But the locals are not impressed. They ask very pointed questions. They want to know the source of his words and deeds. They question the wisdom that has been given to him.

You who have read the Gospel to this point know the answers to their questions. But Jesus' townspeople are limited by their own narrow experience and fixed ideas. They know his family and live in his town and simply cannot believe there is anything significant about him. They describe him using the Greek word *téktōn*, which is traditionally translated as "carpenter." The word means a craftsman who works with wood or metal. Such craftsmen would have produced doors, window frames and other wooden or metallic objects. Jesus and his family would probably have been well-to-do, but would have been regarded as socially inferior to the educated class of religious leaders. In simple terms, the local people think that Jesus is getting above his station with all the recent publicity and that there is really nothing to it or to him. He is no different to themselves. They believe that in trying to move beyond his social standing he is bringing dishonour to his family and so they take offence at him.

Jesus' reply about a prophet not having honour in his home place may well be a proverb which Mark and the other Synoptic evangelists (Matthew 13:57 and Luke 4:24) have re-worked for their own use. Mark's version is very pointed. Jesus is not only rejected by his home town, but by his natural family and relatives. In this way Mark reminds us of the way Jesus' family has already treated him and of the need to create a new family of disciples.

The effect of their rejection is that Jesus is unable to work any significant miracle in Nazareth. Jesus' miracles require faith and this is lacking in Nazareth. Mark is refreshingly direct. He says that Jesus "could not" work miracles in Nazareth. Yet, once said, Mark softens this conclusion and says that Jesus touched some people and brought wholeness into their lives. However, for Mark these are not miracles in the sense of what we have seen when people believe in Jesus. The overall effect on Jesus is that he is "amazed" at the Nazarenes' lack of faith. "Amazement" is often the faith response by people to Jesus' miracles. Now Jesus is "amazed" at unbelief in Nazareth.

Coming back for another look

Read the Gospel again later in the week and think about the following:

• The comments and questions of the Nazarenes highlight something important about Jesus: he was a real human person. He grew up in Nazareth, an ordinary and insignificant little Galilean village. He became a *tékton* and may even have worked on the building of the great Gentile city of Sepphoris about 7km from Nazareth. When he began his mission he did not present himself as some kind of super-hero. Yet, when he did work his miracles, he asked for faith – and this was singularly lacking in Nazareth.

• Sometimes it may seem that the great enemy of faith is doubt. Today's story suggests that it may be "familiarity" or the refusal to believe that God may be working through the person right beside us who is all too well known to us. The Nazarenes were so convinced of their fixed ideas that they could not recognize God's power in Jesus and he could not do a work of power among them. In what way might you be a "Nazarene"?

Fifteenth Sunday in Ordinary Time

15th July 2012

Preparing for Sunday
Read the Gospel: Mark 6:7-13

The explanation

Last week we read about Jesus' difficult and unsuccessful visit to Nazareth. Now Jesus starts a teaching tour of other Galilean villages. Mark's implication is that these villages accept him in a way that Nazareth did not. With this renewed activity Jesus begins to share his mission with the Twelve. Jesus has already chosen them to work with him. Now he puts them to work, sending them out "two by two" armed with his authority to confront the power of evil. He instructs them that they are to travel light. This means no bread, because food will be provided by others' hospitality. It means no (sleeping) bag, as lodging will also be provided. It means no money, for they will be provided for. They can bring a staff, sandals and a single tunic because they will be continually journeying. The other Synoptic evangelists give their own versions of these instructions (Matthew 10:8-10 and Luke 10:4). Such texts remind us that the earliest Christian missionaries travelled light and set themselves apart from the wandering preachers of other religions who brought lots of baggage with them.

Yet Mark is saying something important as he records Jesus' instructions. Jesus is on an urgent missionary journey. The staff and the sandals are the symbols of that journey and so they are appropriate for those who share in his mission. Any other baggage, especially that which might weigh them down and slow up their journey, is not permitted.

Jesus also instructs them about where they are to stay. The issue here is the integrity of the Gospel. If they arrive in a place and then move from house to house seeking better lodging or more friendly company, this would be a counter-witness to the Gospel. Jesus tells them that if they do encounter inhospitality they are to move on from the village. This is exactly what he has done in response to the hostility of Nazareth. Jesus even tells them to shake the dust of such inhospitable places from their feet. Jews returning to the Holy Land would perform this ritual as they left pagan territory so as not to import "uncleanness" with them. It was a gesture which highlighted the godlessness of the pagan land and the holiness of Israel. The Twelve, in performing the same gesture, relegate to the godless world those inhospitable places which have rejected

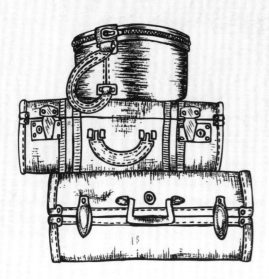

Ironically, the mission of the Twelve is more successful than Jesus' own mission in Nazareth. Yet the Twelve are missionary only to the extent that they are with Jesus, recognize that his authority has been given to them and travel light. At all times they remain his followers.

Coming back for another look

Read the Gospel again later in the week and think about the following:

• This reading points to something fundamental about the Church: it is the new family or community of Jesus which has been entrusted by him to preach the Gospel and to heal people. It is only successful in its ministry when it travels light and discards any baggage which gets in the way of its mission. Since the time of Jesus there have been periods when the Church has travelled "light" and has been truly prophetic in its proclamation of the Gospel. There have been other times when, weighed down with wealth, power and preoccupations with its status, it has failed the Gospel.

The same positive and negative patterns can also be seen in the history of the Irish Church. We can only hope that the deep crisis the Irish Church is going through will lead it to discard anything that gets in the way of Jesus' mission so that the Gospel may be proclaimed anew with prophetic courage and integrity.

the Gospel. In this way the Twelve proclaim the Gospel as Jesus does, with integrity of word and deed.

Following Jesus' instruction, they set out and their mission is successful. Once again when Jesus says that something will happen, it happens exactly as he foretold it. Yet Mark adds some important details. The preaching of the Twelve is so that "all should repent," which is the key missionary goal of Jesus (Mark 1:14-15). The Twelve also heal the sick, something which Jesus has done many times before. Mark adds that they anoint the sick with oil. This was a widespread practice in the Greek world by the time Mark's Gospel was written and now becomes part of the practice of the early Christian Church.

Sixteenth Sunday in Ordinary Time

22nd July 2012

Preparing for Sunday

Read the Gospel: Mark 6:30-34

The explanation

Today we read about the return of the Twelve whom Jesus sent out on mission. Mark calls them "apostles." The word comes from the Greek verb *apostéllō*, which means "to send." They have been sent by Jesus and now are reporting back. But they seem not to have fully understood what has happened. Notice that they tell Jesus about "all that they had done and taught." They have conveniently forgotten that they had gone on mission equipped with Jesus' authority, not their own. They simply have not understood what it means to be sent by Jesus on a mission. Acting on the basis of their own authority, they have not operated as followers.

This may seem a harsh conclusion, but it is part of Mark's hypercritical assessment of their discipleship. Yet he reports them as enthusiastic about the huge response they have received from the people. They have been so engaged in all that they were doing that they did not even have time to eat!

Jesus' response to this popular enthusiasm is to invite them away to a deserted place. As you have seen previously, Jesus is cautious about popular demonstrations of enthusiasm for his message, because they have the capacity to take his mission in the wrong direction. Time apart in a deserted place will help the disciples to understand more fully the mission they now share with him.

So Jesus and his disciples set out across the Sea of Galilee by boat. But the plan fails spectacularly. Seeing the boat, people recognize the passengers and race around the lake to meet Jesus and the disciples when they reach land. Mark says that the people came "from all the towns" around the lake. This is his way of letting us know just how popular Jesus was.

Mark says that Jesus "had compassion on them." In Greek the text reads that "he was moved with compassion for them in his inward parts." In the Hebrew way of associating feelings to parts of the body, compassion was always associated with the womb. In the case of men, the site of compassion was the intestine. While that may seem strange to modern readers, it means that when Jesus sees the people gathered, he has such a feeling of compassion for them that he feels it in the pit of his stomach. It

is a really strong statement of the degree of feeling Jesus has for the people. His reason for such a strong feeling is that the people "were like sheep without a shepherd." This is a phrase that is used in the Old Testament (Numbers 27:17; 1 Kings 22:17; Judith 11:19 and Zechariah 10:2) to describe the people of Israel whenever they suffered from failed or negligent leadership. However, Jesus will not fail and he will not neglect God's people. He will be the true shepherd or leader. He will teach the people and then will go on to feed them (Mark 6:35-44).

Coming back for another look

Read the Gospel again later in the week and think about the following:

• The disciples are so engaged in proclaiming the Gospel that they do not have time to eat! The crowds are so hungry for Jesus' words that they stay all day without eating. There can be no Church without the proclamation of the Word of God. This Gospel story reminds us that hearing the Word of God is just as crucial to being a Catholic as is faith. Similarly there can be no Church without compassionate care for others. The story also reminds us that compassionate care for others, especially the suffering, is as crucial to being a Catholic as is hearing the Word of God.

The biblical phrase "like sheep without a shepherd" describes those suffering from ineffective or defective leadership. It is my view that this phrase could well be used to describe the situation of Catholics in Ireland for some time now. I also believe that Jesus is moved with as a deep a compassion for us today as he was for those people by the Sea of Galilee. He will not fail us or neglect us in this crisis. What do you think?

Seventeenth Sunday in Ordinary Time

29th July 2012

Preparing for Sunday
Read the Gospel: John 6:1-15

The explanation

Last week, we read how Jesus encountered people on the shore of the Sea of Galilee and had compassion for them. If we were to continue reading Mark's Gospel today we would read how he fed the people in the wilderness (Mark 6:35-44). But we do not read Mark's text. Today and for the next four Sundays we read from John 6:1-69. This is the famous "Bread of Life" chapter in the Fourth Gospel. The Synoptic evangelists understand that Jesus celebrated a Passover meal with his disciples on the Thursday night before he died when he gifted them with the Eucharist. John offers a different perspective. For him Jesus celebrated a *farewell* meal on that Thursday night, not a Passover meal. Accordingly in John's telling of the Last Supper there is no account of Jesus' gift of the Eucharist. Rather, John's Eucharistic theology is to be found in John 6:1-69 which we now begin to read.

Today's text is John's account of the feeding of at least five thousand people in the wilderness. This miracle is told by the other evangelists and Matthew and Mark even tell it twice (Matthew 14:13-21; 15:32-39; Mark 6:30-44; 8:1-10 and Luke 9:10-17). It seems there may have been many different versions of this story circulating in the early Church and that John has drawn on a version different to those used by the Synoptic evangelists. Even John's approach to the Eucharist is different. The Synoptic evangelists emphasize Jesus' words and actions in relation to the bread and wine. John emphasizes Jesus' gift of himself.

As we read today's text, Jesus is on the shore of the Sea of Galilee. The people have gathered because they have seen him work a healing miracle or "sign," as John likes to call such miracles. Jesus retreats with his disciples to a mountain. John then adds that the Feast of Passover was near. As you will recall, Passover is the Jewish liturgical celebration of the Exodus event when God liberated the Hebrew slaves from Egypt. Exodus themes will dominate much of John 6, as you will see later.

When Jesus sees the crowd approaching, he knows immediately that they are hungry and asks Philip where they could buy food. He's testing

Philip. Jesus knows exactly what he is going to do, but he wants to see if Philip does. Philip does not and neither does the other disciple, Andrew. They fail to understand that Jesus is the one who will satisfy the people's hunger. Philip and Andrew try to come up with practical but conventional solutions. There are five thousand men present, not counting women and children. According to Philip there is not enough money to feed such a crowd. According to Andrew, there is insufficient food in five loaves and two small fish. Conventional solutions will not feed the people; only Jesus can. Jesus then works the miracle.

Notice something very important in John's account of it. It is *Jesus himself* who shares the food with the people, not the disciples. He is the source of the gift for these hungry people. The miracle produces so much food that twelve baskets of leftovers are gathered. Jesus' command to gather up the leftovers and to waste nothing echoes the Exodus story. On the Exodus trek Moses had commanded the people to do the same with the manna or miraculous bread from heaven given by God in the wilderness (Exodus 16:19). This manna theme will appear again in John 6, as you will see later on.

As always the people are ecstatic about the miracle. They identify Jesus as a prophet and want to make him king. As you have seen before, Jesus is cautious about such enthusiasm based on his miracles or "signs." He is truly a king, but not in the way the people think. His response is to withdraw by himself to the mountain. He will not be their kind of king.

Coming back for another look

Read the Gospel again later in the week and think about the following:

- Jesus' miraculous gift of food was a "sign" of his true identity. The people immediately try to force that identity to serve their own purposes. They want to make him king in order to satisfy their own needs. This text challenges us to see Jesus, not in terms of human glory, but as a sign of God's glory. Jesus has come into the world not to lord it over us in power and authority, but to serve us and to save us for God.

Eighteenth Sunday in Ordinary Time

5th August 2012

Preparing for Sunday
Read the Gospel: John 6:24-35

The explanation

The people do not know where Jesus has gone. They think he might have returned to Capernaum and so they head there. They find him and ask when he had arrived in the village. He doesn't answer their question, but talks about why they had been looking for him in the first place. Whenever he works a miracle it is always a "sign" of his power and authority which invites people to believe in him. When he changed water into wine at Cana (John 2:1-11) and healed the son of a royal official at Capernaum (John 4:46-54), people believed in him. The crowd who now question him have witnessed the miraculous feeding told in last Sunday's reading. It has not resulted in faith – only in full stomachs. The problem is that the people seek ordinary food that "perishes." Again there is an echo here of the Exodus story of the heavenly manna that "bred worms and became foul" overnight (Exodus 16:20). Jesus, the Son of Man, offers food that "endures for eternal life."

"Son of Man" is a Hebrew or Aramaic idiom used when talking about humanity or self. Jesus uses the phrase of himself here. He says that the Father "has set his seal" on the Son of Man. "To set one's seal" is to mark or identify something as one's own. In this way, Jesus is telling the crowd that God has so marked him.

Jesus tells the crowd that he will give food that endures for eternal life. It is Jesus' gift and as such *it is to be received*. But the crowd have missed the point, because they ask what *they have to do*. In replying, Jesus picks up on their words and uses them in a very different way. All the while the crowd continue to use the same words in their own limited way. This is the technique of misunderstanding that the writer of the Fourth Gospel likes to use. The people tell Jesus that they will only do God's work if Jesus first does so by working a miracle. This is an amazing statement! He has just fed at least 5000 people and the crowd now want another miracle if they are going to believe in him. They want a manna-miracle. God had given their ancestors bread in the wilderness. Could Jesus not do something similar? This is hugely ironic as their request follows on from Jesus' feeding miracle!

The people have chosen to use the manna story to make their point, now Jesus uses it to make his point, directly and assertively. It is not Moses who gives the gift of bread; it is Jesus' Father in heaven. This bread is offered now, in the present; it was not available in the past. The bread that he has been speaking of is not some kind of manna-substitute; it is the "true bread from heaven" that God gives to them. In giving this teaching, Jesus may well be re-interpreting Psalm 78:23-25. You should look up that text for yourself in order to appreciate better what Jesus is saying. The bread that Jesus is talking about is bread which "comes down from heaven" and "gives life to the world." This is exactly the same kind of language used in the Fourth Gospel to describe Jesus. He is the Word of God who has come down from heaven and who gives life to the world. You now know what Jesus is talking about. He is talking about himself as the true bread which God the Father is giving the world from heaven. But the crowd's response shows that they still do not understand. They are still thinking about full stomachs! So Jesus has to state it boldly: "I am the bread of life."

Coming back for another look

Read the Gospel again later in the week and think about the following:

• This reading uses rich concepts which have different levels of meaning. "Bread from heaven" is one such concept. It can refer to the manna of the Exodus story or to the Word of God which creates and sustains life. Both food and life are God's gifts to the world. When Jesus says that he is the "bread of life," it means that he is God's life-giving and life-sustaining gift to the world. We do not have to do anything to earn this gift. We only have to trust God and accept it freely.

Nineteenth Sunday in Ordinary Time

12th August 2012

Preparing for Sunday
Read the Gospel: John 6:41-51

The explanation

Jesus has declared to a crowd of people at Capernaum that he is the "bread of life." Today's reading picks up on their response, which is one of utter disbelief. Notice how the writer of the Fourth Gospel refers now to the crowd as "the Jews." While not very politically correct by our standards, the writer uses this phrase to describe those Jewish people who resist Jesus' message. These "complain" about him because of what he has said. This is the same verb used in the Septuagint (or Greek translation of the Old Testament) to describe the Exodus Israelites' grumbling in the wilderness (Exodus 15:24; 16:2.7.12 and Numbers 14:2.27). The crowd who resist Jesus shows the same stubbornness as their ancestors. They find it difficult to accept that Jesus has "come down from heaven." This idea is mentioned five times in John 6. The Exodus manna came from heaven. But Jesus is the true bread descended from heaven which is God's gift to the world. The people reject this because

they claim to know Jesus' parentage. Again the writer is playing with the idea of misunderstanding. They reject Jesus because they claim to know his (human) origins. In fact, they are oblivious to his true origins.

Jesus tells the crowd to stop their complaining. Yet instead of dealing with their issues, he talks about two important themes – about how God draws people to Jesus and about the resurrection on the last day. In doing so he quotes the biblical prophets Isaiah and Jeremiah. In this way Jesus gathers a list of witnesses (God, Isaiah and Jeremiah) who bear testimony to the truth of what he is saying. For Jesus, God is offering a precious teaching to the world. But only those who hear what God is saying and listen to that message will come to Jesus. Jesus is telling the crowd that God is teaching them something, but since they do not listen, they learn nothing. Yet even those who do learn from the Father have never seen him. It is only through Jesus that one can come to the Father, hear God's teaching and learn.

The final section of the reading begins with Jesus' expression "very truly I tell you," which always signals an important statement to follow.

The Year of the Suffering Servant

The bread that he has been talking about is his "flesh" which he will give "for the life of the world." The word flesh has a number of meanings. The Word became flesh in the mystery of the Incarnation out of love for humankind. Out of that same love Jesus will give up his flesh, his body, his life, by dying on the cross. Finally, the idea of eating Jesus' flesh prepares the way for his teaching on the Eucharist, which is to be found in next Sunday's reading.

Coming back for another look

Read the Gospel again later in the week and think about the following:

• As a preacher I do not look forward to these Sundays in Year B when John 6 is read. The text is a rich tapestry of highly complex theological concepts and biblical allusions. Like many preachers, I am challenged both to understand the text and to preach it confidently. This is easier said than done!

Yet when we get past the conceptual complexity and the wealth of biblical allusion, the text says something that is both simple and profound. God, whom we have never seen, loves us. The consequence of the Father's love is his desire that we live forever in his presence. It was out of this amazing love for us that God sent Jesus into the world. All we have to do is come to Jesus in faith and receive what he offers with trust, and that which God desires for us will happen.

And so it is here too. Jesus re-states that he is the bread of life. The crowd's ancestors, whom Jesus calls "your ancestors," certainly ate manna but they eventually died. The Bible links their deaths to their complaining and unbelief (Numbers 14:21-23 and Deuteronomy 1:35). On the other hand, those who eat the bread that Jesus offers will not only be satisfied but will receive the gift of eternal life. Jesus takes the idea of eating one step further. He re-states that he is the "living bread that came down from heaven" and then adds that only by eating this bread can a person live forever.

He finishes with a dramatic and shocking twist.

Twentieth Sunday in Ordinary Time

19th August 2012

Preparing for Sunday
Read the Gospel: John 6:51-58

The explanation

While John 6 has rich theological and biblical content, its text is quite dense and not always easy to understand. We begin today's reading with the final verse from last Sunday's Gospel. Jesus has identified his own flesh with "the living bread that came down from heaven" and has insisted that only those who eat this bread will live forever. It is a dramatic and shocking statement. Today we hear the crowd's response to it. As long as Jesus described himself as "bread of life," it was possible for the crowd to hear his teaching. Now that he starts to talk of himself as "flesh" that people must eat, the crowd respond with shock and horror. Jesus' response is to offer a solemn teaching beginning with "very truly I tell you," which always signals an important statement to follow. Jesus' language becomes even more explicit. Not only does he talk of someone eating his flesh but now he adds the idea of someone drinking his blood. Both are required for eternal life. The language is difficult but it is obvious to the Christian reader that Jesus is talking about the Eucharist. It is by participation in the Eucharist that Jesus' followers will receive his gift of life.

Notice what the writer of the Fourth Gospel is doing here. Jesus' audience is no longer the crowd at Capernaum but those for whom the evangelist wrote the Gospel. This is another technique used frequently by the writer as events in the life of Jesus and in the life of the writer's own community are presented at the same time. Other examples of this technique can be found in John 3:31-36 and 9:18-23. As I noted before, the writer of the Fourth Gospel does not focus on the bread and wine of the Eucharist but on Jesus' total gift of himself ("flesh" and "blood") which happens at the Eucharist.

Jesus re-states his teaching. He no longer talks about himself in the third person, using the title "Son of Man," but speaks directly in the first person, using the pronoun "I." Jesus will raise on the last day all those who eat his flesh and drink his blood. In John 6:40, Jesus says that he will raise on the last day all those who see the Son and believe in him. We didn't read this text at Mass in the last few weeks. You might look it up for yourself as it is important here. For the writer of the Fourth Gospel, the decisions to believe in Jesus and to participate in the Eucharist go together. They cannot be separated. For the evangelist, participation in the Eucharist is the way by which the believer enters into a relationship with Jesus. Notice that Jesus says that those who eat his flesh and drink his blood "abide" in him. But since Jesus shares in God's life, those who "eat" him will share in God's life also.

In the final verse of today's reading, Jesus concludes his teaching on the bread of life. His emphatic message is that whoever eats the bread from heaven that he offers will live forever. We don't read John 6:59 in today's text. I don't know why it has been excluded as it is the evangelist's own conclusion to the "Bread of Life" discourse. Look it up for yourself. It tells us that the whole dialogue between Jesus and the crowd took place "in the synagogue at Capernaum."

Coming back for another look

Read the Gospel again later in the week and think about the following:

• Recent statistics show that the percentage of Catholics in Ireland who "go to Sunday Mass" is in decline. It is most dramatically so in Dublin and in other cities. This same pattern is to be found in many other cities across Western Europe. I'm sure there are several complex reasons for this pattern – secularism, disillusionment, anger with the Church and loss of faith. When Ireland was a "Catholic" country, why did most Catholics "go to Mass"? Was it out of the conviction of faith? Or was it out of custom or culture or coercion?

John's Gospel places a challenge before us who participate in the Eucharist. Our only reason for doing so is because we have personally chosen to be in relationship with Jesus and to follow his teaching, no matter how difficult.

Twenty First Sunday in Ordinary Time

26th August 2012

Preparing for Sunday
Read the Gospel: John 6:60-69

The explanation

Over the past four Sundays we have read Jesus' discourse on the bread of life. Last week we read how the crowd responded to it in shock and rejected it out of hand. Today we read of the response by Jesus' own disciples. They too are shocked at what Jesus has just said and reject his teaching as difficult and unacceptable.

Notice that the evangelist describes the disciples as "complaining" about Jesus' teaching. You will recall that this is the same verb used of the crowd and of the Exodus Israelites. As he did with the crowd, Jesus throws down a challenge to his followers. He first asks if his teaching has offended them and then goes on to ask if his return to the Father will also offend them. You will recall that for the Fourth Gospel, Jesus' death, resurrection and return to the Father is a single event that takes place at Golgotha. So Jesus is challenging them that if they find his teaching on the bread of life offensive, will they also find his death, resurrection and ascension offensive? The fact that Jesus will return to the Father reminds us that he has come from the Father. Might the disciples be offended by this too?

He now gives them a further teaching. The disciples, just like "the Jews" (as understood in the context of the Fourth Gospel), have not understood Jesus' teaching. When he talks of flesh, they think of Jesus' own flesh and not of "the Word made flesh." Once again Jesus is talking of the Eucharist. He is not asking the disciples to eat flesh and drink blood. He is asking them to go beyond their limited understanding of life and to embrace him fully along with his teaching on the Eucharist. But some of them do not believe and Jesus knows it. The true disciple must choose to believe in Jesus and accept him as a gift offered graciously by God.

Jesus' declaration that there are those who do not believe triggers a crisis. "Many disciples" make their decision about him immediately and walk away. So he throws down the challenge to the Twelve. Will they walk too? Will they accept the gift God is offering them, or will they reject it? Notice that the evangelist uses the term "the Twelve." It is a rare

The Year of the Suffering Servant

word in the Fourth Gospel (John 6:67.70-71 and 20:24). The Synoptic Gospels use it more frequently. It may well be that the evangelist is assuming that his readers are familiar with the call of the Twelve (which he does not recount) and of Peter's leadership from other traditions outside his Gospel. In any case, this scene in John 6:66-69 is the Fourth Gospel's version of Peter's confession at Caesarea Philippi (Matthew 16:13-20 and Mark 8:27-33). Peter makes his choice and it is one *for* Jesus. He has listened to Jesus' teaching on the bread of life and he knows that Jesus has "the words of eternal life." He speaks also for the rest of the Twelve and declares that they both know and believe that Jesus is "the Holy One of God." This is the only place in the Fourth Gospel where Jesus is so described. Look up John 10:36 for yourself. There Jesus is described as "the one whom the Father has sanctified and sent into the world." Jesus is God's holy agent sent into the world and this is what Peter confesses here.

Coming back for another look

Read the Gospel again later in the week and think about the following:

• The Fourth Gospel's theology of the Eucharist is quite different from that of the Synoptic evangelists who link it to the Passover meal at the Last Supper. It is a theology which offers a challenging alternative perspective to the contemporary Eucharistic theology and practice of the Church (Catholic, Protestant and Orthodox). It poses a particular challenge to any Eucharistic theology that elevates the role of the presider of the Eucharist over that of other believers.

The writer of the Fourth Gospel has chosen to present his Eucharistic theology in the context of Jesus' "Bread of Life" discourse. In doing so the evangelist presents the Eucharist as Jesus' direct personal gift to each believer who makes the choice for him in faith and not to any hierarchical group or institution. This is not to say that the more hierarchical and institutional perspective of the Synoptic evangelists should be disregarded. The Church needs both.

Twenty Second Sunday in Ordinary Time

2nd September 2012

Preparing for Sunday
Read the Gospel: Mark 7:1-8.14-15.21-23

The explanation

Today we return to Mark's Gospel. The Pharisees and scribes gather around Jesus and his disciples. The mood is ominous and conflict is not far away. You will recall that the Pharisees were a group of very devout Jews who observed relentlessly all the commandments of the Law and that the scribes were the Jewish theologians or scripture scholars who offered regular teaching based on their interpretation of the sacred texts. They get into an argument about the fact that some of Jesus' disciples eat with unwashed hands. It is important to note that it is "some of his disciples" who are not washing their hands. These disciples are following strict Jewish practice, while clearly others are not. You can recognize easily that Mark's audience is Gentile, as he has to explain Jewish rituals around cleanliness issues. Mark does not criticize these ritual practices. He merely lists them as practices followed by the Pharisees, all the Jews and some of Jesus' disciples.

However, Mark is not altogether factual. "All the Jews" did not follow such ritual practices, only the followers of Pharisees. You might check out for yourself Leviticus 11-15 where the laws on what is clean and unclean are to be found. Because of its special relationship with God, Israel considered itself and its land to be holy and should therefore keep away from that which was unclean or profane. The Pharisees were extremely concerned that all Jews would remain holy, especially since Palestine in the first century AD was a mixed society of Jew and Gentile and contamination by "uncleanness" was always possible. The Pharisees based their practice not just on Leviticus 11-15 but also on an ancient unwritten tradition called the "tradition of the elders." In effect, the Pharisees are checking out the attitude of Jesus and his disciples to these ancient traditional practices.

Jesus' response is highly confrontational as he questions the ancient traditions by quoting from the Old Testament (Isaiah 29:13). In using this quotation, Jesus highlights what is most important in a person's relationship with God. It is the person's "heart" (or moral centre from which everything comes) that is important – more important than mere "human traditions." Jesus also uses the quotation from Isaiah to declare that the Pharisees have turned God's commandments into mere human rules and regulations. In doing so, they have reduced the Jewish religion to vain worship of God.

Now Jesus gathers the people together who have been following the confrontation. It is almost like he is offering them a parable as he begins with "listen to me, all of you and understand." He gives them his own teaching on what is "clean" and "unclean." Nothing that goes into a person (food) creates uncleanness.

The Pharisees and scribes most certainly hear this as a provocation as Jesus seems to be setting aside their traditions around kosher (ritually fit) food. For Jesus, it is what comes out of a person's heart (evil intentions) that makes a person unclean. Mark's list of evil intentions is traditionally Jewish. The Torah (the first five books of the Jewish Scriptures) explicitly forbids the first nine items in the list (fornication, theft, murder, adultery, avarice, malice, deceit, indecency and envy). The last three items (slander, pride and foolishness) seem very small in comparison to the first nine. But these are critical issues for Mark. His community was sorely divided in itself and it may well be that Mark regarded slander, pride and foolishness to be the root causes of such divisions.

In this controversy story, Mark highlights Jesus'

teaching that it is moral impurity that defiles a person, not ritual impurity. While Jesus insists that moral cleanness or holiness is more important than ritual holiness, Jesus does not reject the Jewish scriptures. Rather, in the best tradition of the prophets, he argues that holiness is a matter of the "heart." Put simply, if you want to know if people are holy and in a good relationship with God, then check out what comes out of their hearts.

Coming back for another look

Read the Gospel again later in the week and think about the following:

- The temptation to religious legalism and control which Jesus challenges in his own religion have happened in our Church and can still happen today. Yet it is worse today, for such is done in Jesus' name. It is far easier for us to follow external ritual practices than to change our hearts, mind-sets, attitudes and behaviour. This is a Gospel reading that demands much honest reflection by all in the Church.

Twenty Third Sunday in Ordinary Time

9th September 2012

Preparing for Sunday
Read the Gospel: Mark 7:31-37

The explanation

Jesus has left the Holy Land of Israel and is travelling in Gentile territory. He has returned from Tyre via Sidon, which were two cities in Phoenicia (now part of modern Lebanon), and travels through non-Jewish territory known as the Decapolis. The name Decapolis comes from the Greek words *déka* ("ten") and *pólis* ("city") and refers to a group of ten cities that were Greek and Roman in culture and language. Nine of the cities were located in what is today modern Jordan, while one of them (Beth Shean) is located in modern Israel.

According to the Synoptic evangelists, the Decapolis was one of the few Gentile regions in which Jesus travelled and ministered. You might find it helpful to get a map of Palestine in New Testament times. Your Bible should have one. Locate Tyre and Sidon for yourself and then find the region of the Decapolis. You will easily see that Jesus' journey is a little odd in that it is not the most direct way back to the Holy Land and to Galilee.

It is on this trip through the Decapolis that he heals the man who has both a hearing and speech impediment. Mark gives the details about Jesus' travels in order to remind his readers (and us) that the man who is healed is a Gentile, as are those who bring him to Jesus. He takes the man aside and then performs a series of physical actions. He puts his fingers in the man's ears. He touches the man's tongue with his own spittle. Finally, speaking in Aramaic, he gives the command ephphata! ("be opened!"). Notice how Mark translates Jesus' Aramaic for his readers who would have been unfamiliar with it.

To those witnessing Jesus' actions, it must seem like some kind of magic spell. The gestures are those of typical magicians of the time and the phrase in Aramaic would have sounded like the gibberish of a magic spell to them. But Jesus is no magician. Rather, he summons up God's power and uses his own authority to command the healing of the hearing and speech impediment.

The result of Jesus' actions is immediate. The man's ears are "opened" and the "bond of his tongue was loosened." Now the man can speak clearly. The miracle is done in private and Jesus asks those who brought the man to him to keep it so. This again highlights Jesus' caution about over-enthusiastic responses to his miracles that miss the point of his mission.

If Jesus hopes they will listen to him, it is in vain. They are "absolutely overwhelmed" by the miracle and tell the story everywhere and acclaim that "he has done all things well; he made the deaf hear and the dumb speak." This is an allusion to Isaiah 35:5-6. This text speaks of a time when Israel's Messiah would bring healing and freedom for God's people. Mark is proclaiming clearly that the time of the Messiah has arrived with Jesus who will offer healing and freedom not just to the Jewish people, but to Gentiles as well. More than that, Mark is also suggesting that it is the Gentiles who first publicly recognize who and what Jesus might be, albeit in a limited way.

Coming back for another look

Read the Gospel again later in the week and think about the following:

• The man in this story must be lonely and isolated. He cannot hear and he cannot speak. For him communication is extremely limited. He is unable to communicate his own thoughts and feelings freely and with ease. By his words and touch, Jesus gifts him with all he needs for meaningful human communication. In some ways this man

represents all Christian believers. We need Jesus to open our ears to God's life-giving Word. We also need Jesus to gift us with courageous speech to proclaim our faith.

• Jesus' disciples also have hearing and speech impediments. They are deaf to what Jesus is telling them and so they are unable to speak out and give witness to the Gospel. Like the Gentile man in today's reading, they also need to be healed by Jesus. But this healing will not come until they have journeyed with him to Jerusalem and until they have faced Golgotha and the empty tomb.

Twenty Fourth Sunday in Ordinary Time

16th September 2012

Preparing for Sunday
Read the Gospel: Mark 8:27-35

The explanation

As we read today's text we move from the section of Mark's Gospel dealing with his ministry in Galilee (Mark 1:14–8:30) to that dealing with his journey to Jerusalem (Mark 8:31–10:52). Just before Jesus sets out for Jerusalem he heals a blind man at Bethsaida (Mark 8:22-26). We don't read this text on the Sundays in Year B, so you might read it for yourself. Just before the end of the journey, at Jericho, he heals blind Bartimaeus (Mark 10:46-52). This is a story we will read on the Thirtieth Sunday in Ordinary Time. The healing of these two blind men suggests that the journey to Jerusalem is about blindness – the disciples' blindness to Jesus' identity and mission. It will be a difficult trip for all concerned. Yet before he heads south, he travels north to the villages surrounding Caesarea Philippi.

On the way there he puts a key question to them: "Who do people say that I am?" You already know that Jesus' identity is a fundamental issue in Mark's

You are the Christ

Gospel. You also know that from the very beginning of the Gospel Mark has identified Jesus as Messiah and Son of God (Mark 1:1). The disciples have not recognized his true identity but have struggled to make sense of it (Mark 4:41), as have the people of Galilee (Mark 6:14-15). Now, before the journey to Jerusalem and the fate that awaits him there, Jesus attempts to get the disciples to acknowledge his true identity.

In response to his question they list what people are saying about him. He is John the Baptizer returned from the dead. He is Elijah returned from heaven. He is a prophet. Now he asks them directly: "Who do you say that I am?" Peter seems to give the right answer, for he says: "You are the Christ (or Messiah)." It sounds right. The only problem is that Peter is identifying Jesus with the royal, conventional and powerful Messiah of Jewish expectation. Peter still cannot recognize Jesus as the Suffering Messiah.

Now Jesus begins to talk about what lies ahead of him in Jerusalem. Mark offers three texts (Mark 8:31-33; 9:30-32 and 10:32-34) that are known as the Passion Predictions. It is the beginning of Jesus' effort to get the disciples to see that he is not a powerful and glorious Messiah, but one who will suffer and die. In response, Peter "remonstrates" with Jesus. The Greek text reads that Peter "took hold" of Jesus. This earns him the sharpest rebuke ever given by Jesus to anyone. Jesus calls Peter "Satan"! There may well be a play on the Hebrew word *sātān*, which means a "stumbling block." If Peter causes Jesus to stumble in fulfilling God's plan, then he will play into the hands of Satan. What Jesus wants is that Peter and the other disciples "get behind" him to support and follow him - not get in his way. He needs the disciples to think not in terms of limited expectations (human thinking), but in terms of the mission (divine thinking). A terrible

fate awaits Jesus. Similarly, a difficult future lies in store for those who follow him as disciples.

In this context, Jesus sets out the conditions for being a disciple. It involves "denying oneself" and "taking up the cross" and following Jesus. Denial of self does not mean small, simple Lenten penances. It means placing the demands of discipleship above everything else in one's life. "Taking up the cross" means a willingness to follow Jesus in the midst of suffering and even to the point of death.

The final sentence of today's reading is a paradox. Jesus is saying that those who give everything to preserve their earthly life could end up losing eternal life while those who are prepared to lose their earthly life for the sake of the Gospel will end up saving their eternal life. These are not the easiest words of Jesus found in the Gospel!

Coming back for another look

Read the Gospel again later in the week and think about the following:

- Today's text contains some very hard words directed at Peter, who recognizes, albeit incompletely, that Jesus is the Messiah. But he cannot face the idea that Jesus must face a horrible death. It is simply unthinkable for Peter. We can identify with him, as nobody wants to see a loved one or friend suffer. Yet every time suffering comes into our lives, we need to hear Jesus words, "get behind me," and renew our discipleship and follow him along the way.

Twenty Fifth Sunday in Ordinary Time

23rd September 2012

Preparing for Sunday
Read the Gospel: Mark 9:30-37

The explanation

Jesus and his disciples are journeying through Galilee towards Jerusalem. This is a journey on which Jesus will try to get them to understand what true discipleship means. Jesus doesn't want the local people to know their whereabouts as he wants to focus on the difficult task in hand. He is explicit about his fate. He will be handed over to others who will kill him and three days later he will rise again.

The disciples do not understand what he is saying and they are "afraid to ask him about it." You will recall that, for Mark, fear corrodes and destroys discipleship. It is doing its destructive work yet again. The disciples still think of Jesus as the conventional and powerful Jewish Messiah. They simply cannot accept him as he describes himself, God's Suffering Messiah.

They arrive at Capernaum and enter a house. Suddenly we realise that they had been arguing among themselves as they journeyed along. Jesus was aware of it, but had said nothing. When he asks what they were arguing about, he is met with sullen silence. As always, Mark refuses to let them off the hook. He tells us what they had being arguing about. They had been discussing who among them was the greatest. Still thinking in terms of the conventional Jewish Messiah, they were arguing as to who would have status and power in the new messianic kingdom. Their mentality is completely at odds with what Jesus was trying to teach them on the road.

Mark tells us that Jesus now sits down. This is the position taken up by a teacher who is about to instruct students. He calls the Twelve to him and offers an instruction in two parts. The first part sets out Jesus' understanding of the leadership that is to be exercised in his kingdom. The person who desires to be first must be last and servant of the others. The Twelve think that Jesus will be a glorious Messiah. He tells them he will be a Suffering Messiah. The Twelve think in terms of powerful and prestigious positions in the messianic kingdom. He tells them that being last and servant of all is what counts. The cross that awaits them in Jerusalem reverses all human measurements of success and reveals the

The Year of the Suffering Servant

true values of Jesus' kingdom. This is the painful lesson they must learn.

Jesus then offers the second part of his instruction in a highly dramatic fashion. He sets a child in front of them. He then wraps his arms around the child and identifies the child with himself. The one that welcomes (or in Greek "receives") the child welcomes Jesus and the one that welcomes Jesus welcomes the Father. Children in first century Palestine had no status, power or value. If an adult were to "welcome" or "receive" a child (as an equal) it would mean turning social and cultural values upside down. It would mean putting aside any ideas of self-importance or adult status. But this is what Jesus requires of the Twelve. They must be ready to be the servants of all, as Jesus is, even to the point of his giving his life for others.

Another possible understanding of Jesus' action is that a child is always open to new experiences. Jesus chooses the child as a symbol of those followers who will receive him and his teaching with childlike openness. The Twelve have not yet learned to do this and must journey further.

Coming back for another look

Read the Gospel again later in the week and think about the following:

•   In my opinion the Catholic Church across the world, and most especially in Ireland, needs to reflect long and hard on Jesus' journey to Jerusalem

and on his teaching about discipleship. After many centuries of persecution, Christianity became the official religion of the Roman Empire in the early fourth century AD and the Church got hopelessly entangled in the trappings of Roman power, wealth and status. These trappings hold a seductive lure on the Church today as some Church leaders still put an emphasis on power, dress, titles, honours and status that is not in accord with the Gospel.

The scandals that have rocked the Church may well purify it and free it from the trappings Jesus warns of. Some Church leaders in Ireland talk about the Church becoming more "humble." If "humble" means receiving Jesus and his teaching as he hoped the Twelve would, then it will be an exciting new beginning for us. But it will not be without pain.

Twenty Sixth Sunday in Ordinary Time

30th September 2012

Preparing for Sunday
Read the Gospel: Mark 9:38-43.45.47-48

The explanation

As Jesus and his disciples continue their journey to Jerusalem, John the son of Zebedee (and brother of James) speaks up. Along with Peter they are Jesus' "inner core" of disciples within the Twelve. The issue is that they have come across a man casting out demons in Jesus' name and they have stopped him because he was not one of them. The Greek text reads: "because he did not follow *us.*" Jesus has tried to teach his disciples about the need for service and receptivity, as you read in last week's reading. John is complaining, not because this unknown man acted in Jesus' name, but because the man was not following the *Twelve!*

John may well expect a word of praise from Jesus, who must be completely exasperated by now. If he is, he does not show it. He simply gives John a mild rebuke. For Jesus anyone who acts in his name should never be stopped. He does not mind his name being used for a good purpose. If this man was prepared to act in Jesus' name, then he was not opposed to Jesus. In fact, the man has shown the two values Jesus has been trying to teach the disciples – service of others and receptivity to his message. The Twelve have yet to learn what it means to be a follower of Jesus as "receptive servant."

Jesus' reply to John is clear – all who encounter Jesus will have to make a fundamental decision about him. Either they are for him or against him. Jesus then clarifies what he is saying by giving an example. If someone from outside the group of disciples shows them a simple act of kindness, such as giving them a cup of water, that person will be rewarded for the good they do. True disciples of Jesus will always rejoice when others are served and will never seek privilege and power for themselves. They will rejoice when goodness is done, even if it is not a disciple who does it.

The first part of the reading deals with goodness done *from outside the community of disciples*. The second part deals with evil done *within the community of disciples*. Jesus talks of "little ones" who are "scandalized." These "little ones" are either children or vulnerable people. The word "scandalized" comes from a Greek word meaning "to cause to sin" through bad example or exploitative behaviour. Jesus is talking about more powerful people within the community of disciples who cause weaker members to sin through exploitation. Jesus uses dramatic and exaggerated speech to make his point. If it were better for someone powerful to suffer a guaranteed death by drowning (that is "thrown into the sea with a great millstone around his neck"), how much more terrible the punishment for those who cause weaker members of the community to sin!

Now Jesus uses a stark, drastic and somewhat chilling example. He is drawing on the image of radical surgery used to remove a diseased organ (hand, foot, and eye) in order to save the whole body. Jesus says that such surgery is better than entering Gehenna whole but diseased by sin. Gehenna comes from the Greek word *géenna*, which is the equivalent for the Hebrew *Ge Hinnom*, meaning the "Valley of Hinnom." This was a valley on the western side of Jerusalem and had a gruesome history. Before 1000 BC the Canaanite population of the city used to sacrifice babies there as burnt offerings to the god Moloch. In Jesus' day it was the place where Jerusalem's municipal rubbish was constantly burnt. With these associations, Gehenna eventually became a Jewish metaphor for Hell with its supposed eternal fire.

What exactly might Jesus be saying using such dramatic and forceful language? He is emphasizing that life in the Kingdom of God is something of supreme importance. It is so important that his disciples must do everything possible not to lose it.

Coming back for another look

Read the Gospel again later in the week and think about the following:

•   Jesus' talk of amputations and hellfire is not easy for us to hear. His original audience understood well that he was not talking literally but in metaphors, and we need to understand this too. However, his challenge to us is much tougher than his metaphors. Is discipleship something precious to you? Or is it merely something cultural? Would you easily set it aside when the going gets tough? Discipleship that can be easily set aside is not what Jesus is calling for.

Preparing for Sunday
Read the Gospel: Mark 10:2-16

The explanation

Jesus and his disciples are still on their journey to Jerusalem. Crowds gather around him and he begins to each them. Then some Pharisees question him about divorce. Mark says that they were trying to "test" him. They may well know his position already and want to show him up as opposing the Jewish law, which allowed for divorce. You should read Deuteronomy 24:1-4 for yourself in order to understand the context for today's reading. Notice that Jewish law only permits *a man to divorce his wife.* It does not permit a wife to divorce her husband. Notice also that the law regulates divorce, but does not state explicitly what the grounds for divorce actually are. It makes a vague reference to the man finding something "objectionable" about his wife. So it was that Jewish teachers argued over what the precise legal grounds for a divorce actually were.

Jesus is ready for the Pharisees. He asks them what Moses "commanded." They reply that Moses "allowed" for divorce. So Jesus gets the Pharisees to admit that divorce was allowed by Moses, but not commanded by him. In simple terms, Moses had accepted that divorce was a fact of life and then regulated it to protect the woman's rights. So for Jesus, divorce is a concession that Moses allowed due to the man's "hardness of heart." But the Kingdom of God (God's rule) is opposed to any hardness of heart.

Jesus then offers his teaching based on the original will of the Creator found in Genesis 1-2. For Jesus, the law of Moses did nothing more than minimize the harm done to the wife in a hard-hearted process biased in favour of the husband. Against this, Jesus understands the marriage relationship between a man and a woman as an *indivisible relationship* willed by God from the dawn of creation. Jesus centres his public teaching on Genesis1-2, which is also part of the Jewish law.

Then later, "in the house," he offers a private teaching to the disciples. For Jesus, divorce and remarriage violate the commandment against adultery. Notice that Jesus refers also to a situation where a woman divorces her husband. This could not happen under the Jewish law, but could under Roman law, which operated in Mark's day. This is Mark's way of taking Jesus' basic teaching and applying it to the changed context of the Christian community 40 years later. Jesus' teaching remains as demanding and as countercultural today as it was in his own time. But in giving this teaching Jesus is showing that everything he has been teaching his disciples about the cross, service and discipleship is not just theoretical, but something that is required in one of the most fundamental of human relationships.

The final part of today's reading is about Jesus and children. People bring children to Jesus to touch them. Yet again the disciples get it wrong. Like some kind of security detail, they shoo the people away. The Greek text says that they "rebuke" the people. The disciples still do not understand Jesus and have already forgotten his words about receiving children. Jesus is indignant. He asks that the children be allowed come to him. For Jesus, children model how all disciples are to be open to God's gifts, in particular the gift of the Kingdom. This gift can only be received with childlike receptivity.

His final words are a warning to the disciples. They (as adults) will only be able to enter the Kingdom if they accept it as a pure gift as a child would. The scene ends with Jesus, not just touching the children, but blessing them.

Coming back for another look

Read the Gospel again later in the week and think about the following:

• Many people listening to this reading may be in second unions or have family members in such circumstances. Jesus' words are not easy and remain a painful challenge. Yet they must be understood in context of the first century AD. Life expectancy was half of what it is today in the Western world. Most marriages ended naturally with the death of one of the spouses after about 20 years. The first generation of Christians (and Jesus himself) believed the world would end in their own lifetime. In this context the issue of second marriages seemed unreal. When Matthew, writing 15 years after Mark, gives his account of Jesus' teaching on divorce (Matthew 5:32 and 19:9), he certainly seems to suggest that Jesus allows for divorce in limited circumstances. The various Christian Churches have reflected on these texts, and developed their disciplines differently.

Twenty Eighth Sunday in Ordinary Time

14th October 2012

Preparing for Sunday
Read the Gospel; Mark 10:17-30

The explanation

A man approaches Jesus with energetic enthusiasm. Going on his knees, he calls Jesus a "good teacher" and asks what he needs to do "to inherit eternal life." It's the wrong question. The man believes that he has to *do something* to enter God's Kingdom and that Jesus will tell him what this is. Jesus doesn't answer the man's question, but addresses the issue at a much deeper level. He reacts negatively at being called "good" and focuses on God's goodness. Jesus then tries to get the man to move away from thinking that he has to *do* something to gain the Kingdom and to focus on God's generosity.

Jesus lists some of the commandments. Notice those he lists. They are all social commandments which deal with a person's relationship with the neighbour. They are commandments which the rich might be tempted to ignore. While the man has kept them all since his youth, he now wants to do something more. There is an emptiness in his life and he wants to fill it. Mark adds a unique detail in telling us that "Jesus, looking at him, loved him." Jesus does not love him because he has kept the commandments. Rather Jesus loves him with the love of God because he is about to call the man into a more intimate and personal relationship with God.

The man is a devout Jew. Jesus now invites him to go further. He calls on him to sell all he owns, give the money to the poor and follow him. Jesus invites him to let go of false security (his wealth) and trust himself to God's total generosity. It is an invitation to move beyond the Jewish law, with its emphasis on fulfilling commandments, to a life centred on relationship with Jesus. But the man is trapped by his wealth and he knows it. He cannot let it go, so he goes away "grieving." Ensnared by his wealth, he lacks the interior freedom to choose Jesus and the Kingdom.

Jesus lets the man go because he does not coerce people into discipleship. Yet he uses the event to point out to the disciples that wealth creates huge difficulties to entering God's Kingdom. They are "perplexed" when they hear his words. They were brought up to believe that wealth was a sign of God's favour and blessing (Deuteronomy 28:1-14 and Job 42:12). Now Jesus tells them that wealth is an obstacle to God.

Then he astounds them with his highly amusing and proverbial image. A camel will get through the eye of a needle more easily than a wealthy person can enter heaven! The disciples can only conclude that salvation is simply impossible. This allows Jesus to make his fundamental point. When the Kingdom of God is looked at from a limited human perspective, then the whole thing seems impossible. But nothing is impossible for God, since God will give to those who wish to enter the Kingdom everything that they need. The rich man balked at the apparent impossibility of entering the Kingdom. But what might have happened if he had trusted that God would give him the capacity to enter it?

Peter, speaking for all the disciples, reminds Jesus that they have left everything to follow him. Jesus' response is to list what the disciples have left behind and then list what they will receive back a hundredfold. Look carefully at the two lists. The word "father" occurs in the first list (of what the disciples have abandoned). It does not occur in the second list (of what they will receive back a hundredfold). As Jesus' disciples, they now have a single Father: God. Notice too that Jesus adds "persecutions" to the second list. This would have struck a chord with Mark's original readers who were suffering terrible persecution because of following Jesus.

Coming back for another look

Read the Gospel again later in the week and think about the following:

- This is not an easy text. If we can only get into God's Kingdom by abandoning everything we love to embrace Jesus' radical lifestyle, then it does seem totally impossible. If Jesus' first followers had done this, the Church would never have survived beyond the first century AD. We need to read Mark's Gospel in the context of the entire New Testament. Other New Testament books explore what Jesus' radical message might mean for settled family-based Christian communities. Nonetheless, we need to hear the Markan Jesus' radical summons to consider our lifestyles in the context of God's generosity.

Twenty Ninth Sunday in Ordinary Time

21st October 2012

Preparing for Sunday
Read the Gospel: Mark 10:35-45

The explanation

On the journey from Galilee to Jerusalem, Jesus makes three predictions about the suffering and death that await him in the city. They are known as the Passion Predictions (Mark 8:31-32; 9:31-32 and 10:32-34). The disciples' reactions to these predictions highlight their blindness to Jesus' identity and their resistance to his message. If you want to understand today's reading, it would be worthwhile reading the disciples' reaction to the Passion Predictions. Peter reacts to the first prediction by rebuking Jesus and earns a sharp retort in return (Mark 8:32-33). The disciples react to the second prediction with a lack of understanding and fear (Mark 9:32).

In today's text James and John react to the third prediction. Having just heard Jesus' graphic description of his fate, they ask for thrones of privilege and power in the Kingdom. They are completely blind to Jesus and simply have failed to hear anything he has been saying. Along with

Peter they are part of Jesus' inner core of disciples. They were with him when he raised Jairus' daughter to life in Capernaum (Mark 5:37) and they saw his glory on the mount of Transfiguration (Mark 9:2). Despite all this, their discipleship is flawed by naked ambition.

Jesus' response, as so often with his disciples, is one of patience. He tries to get James and John to understand the implications of what they have just requested. He uses biblical images. He asks them if they can drink the "cup" that he must drink and undergo the "baptism" he faces. In the Bible the "cup" is often a symbol of the suffering and death that lie ahead for a person. "Baptism" as used here has nothing to do with John the Baptizer's Jordan ritual or with the Christian sacrament. Rather, it means total immersion. In this case Jesus is talking about the total immersion in suffering which awaits him in Jerusalem.

Using these images Jesus asks the two if they are willing to share his fate. They say that they are, but really they don't know what they are agreeing to. Jesus accepts their response and then goes on to say that he cannot offer them the places in the Kingdom that they are seeking. He is going to his fate and, when the moment of his death comes, he will surrender himself in trust and with obedience into the hands of the generous and faithful God. He will die without knowing God's response, but trusting it. James and John will have no guarantees either. They too will have to trust God's fidelity and generosity. So it must be for all who would be Jesus' disciples.

The request made by James and John stirs up jealous resentment and irritation in the other apostles. They also are full of naked ambition and are highly annoyed at the effort of James and John to steal a march on them and to get the best places in the Kingdom. If Jesus is exasperated with the whole lot of them, he doesn't show it. Rather, he responds again with patience. He takes up the issue of how leadership is to be exercised in the Kingdom of God and contrasts it with the request made by James and John. He takes the example of Gentile rulers who "lord it over" their subject people. They so abuse their power that they become "tyrants." Yet this is not the way it is to be in the community of Jesus' disciples. Those who exercise leadership in his community must become servants and slaves of others. In this way those who have leadership capacity must exercise it for the sake of the others in the community.

Coming back for another look

Read the Gospel again later in the week and think about the following:

• This text ends with one of the most important statements in the whole Gospel (Mark 10:45). Pay particular attention to this verse. Jesus offers himself as an example of how leadership must be exercised. He has come not to be served but to serve and he will do this most explicitly by giving "his life as a ransom for many." The Greek word for "ransom" means the price paid to free those held unjustly against their will (slaves, prisoners of war, or kidnapped people). Jesus will free people ensnared by evil through his death. He is not the Messiah of conventional Jewish expectation. He is God's Suffering Messiah. Those who wish to be his disciples need to learn this in order to follow him.

Thirtieth Sunday in Ordinary Time

28th October 2012

Preparing for Sunday
Read the Gospel: Mark 10:46-52

The explanation

Jesus' journey from Galilee to Jerusalem is almost at an end. He has just one more town to pass through, Jericho, which is only 24 km from Jerusalem. You will recall that on his long journey south Jesus has tried to open his disciples' eyes to his true identity and he has attempted to reduce their resistance to his message. He hasn't been completely successful. They are not able to see him clearly as God's Suffering Messiah, nor do they understand much of what he has been teaching them.

Once again Jesus heals a blind man, called Bartimaeus. This healing at the end of the journey corresponds to the healing of the blind man of Bethsaida at the start of the journey (Mark 8:22-26). In between these two miracles Jesus has tried to heal his disciples' spiritual blindness.

Bartimaeus is very likely sitting at the city gates begging as pilgrims pass along on their way to Jerusalem. Notice that Bartimaeus is sitting "by the way (roadside)" while Jesus and his disciples are "on the way" to Jerusalem. Bartimaeus is not one of Jesus' disciples. He is also blind and a beggar. He is a nobody. When he hears that Jesus of Nazareth is among these pilgrims he makes a noisy commotion. He cries out, "Jesus, Son of David, have mercy on me!" "Son of David" is a term used by Jewish people in the first century AD to refer to the Messiah. Jesus would have silenced such a Messianic acclamation during his ministry in Galilee. He doesn't do so now as he is near to Jerusalem where he will be revealed as God's Suffering Messiah.

Bartimaeus recognizes that Jesus can heal him and rescue him from his nothingness. The onlookers try to silence Bartimaeus. They are a barrier between him and Jesus. Again Mark has made it clear that Jesus' own disciples are part of this crowd following him, and it is safe to assume that some of the disciples try to silence Bartimaeus. They have learnt nothing on the road from Galilee. But Bartimaeus' need is great and he will not be silenced.

Jesus' hears his cries and calls for him. Notice what Bartimaeus does. He jumps up and flings off his cloak and goes to Jesus. With these dramatic

experienced the salvation that Jesus offers. Like the foreign woman (Mark 7:24-30) and the father of the epileptic boy (Mark 9:14-29), Bartimaeus has come to Jesus with nothing but his faith and that faith has saved him.

Jesus tells him he can "go." He is free. He no longer has to sit by the roadside begging. But he doesn't go away. On the contrary, he follows Jesus "on the way." Later on in the development of the New Testament, the verb "to follow" Jesus will usually indicate discipleship and conversion. Bartimaeus becomes a disciple and is prepared to follow Jesus to Jerusalem. More than that, he becomes something the other disciples have yet failed to become – a model of discipleship and faith.

gestures he shows his faith in Jesus. His actions equal those of Jesus' first disciples in Galilee. They let go of their trades, possessions and families to follow Jesus.

In most of Mark's miracles stories, the one to be healed requests a healing. "What do you want me to do for you?" Jesus asks him. His answer is clear: "My teacher, let me see again." This is exactly the same question that Jesus put to James and John (which we read last Sunday). In their case they wanted seats of power and privilege and so showed themselves to be blinded by ambition. Bartimaeus asks to "see again." Unlike James and John, Bartimaeus wants to see Jesus and understand him. He wants that which the very disciples of Jesus have failed to seek. Jesus tells him to go, as his faith has "made him well." The Greek text says that Bartimaeus' faith has "saved" him. He has received his sight back, but he has also

Coming back for another look

Read the Gospel again later in the week and think about the following:

- Bartimaeus models for us the kind of discipleship that Jesus is looking for. He believes in Jesus and will not be silenced. It is not easy to be a public committed, practicing Catholic in Ireland today. There are those in our secular and increasingly intolerant society who would gladly silence us. That is why like Bartimaeus we need to cry out all the more – "Son of David, have mercy on us!"

Thirty First Sunday in Ordinary Time

4th November 2012

Preparing for Sunday

Read the Gospel: Mark 12:28-34

The explanation

Jesus' journey from Galilee to Jerusalem is over. Mark understands that Jesus comes to Jerusalem only once in his life and now tells what happened in the last week of his life. Mark 11:1–14:11 covers Jesus' first four days in the city (Sunday to Wednesday) while Mark 14:12–16:20 covers his last days there (Thursday to Sunday). We do not read all the week's events at the Sunday Eucharist in Year B. Jesus' triumphal entry into Jerusalem on the Sunday of that week (Mark 11:1-10) is read on Passion Sunday of Year B in the ceremony of the blessing of the palms. The events which take place on Monday – the barren fig-tree (Mark 11:12-14) and the cleansing of the Temple (Mark 11:15-19) – are not read in Year B. Tuesday sees Jesus teaching in the Temple (Mark 12:1-44). Today we read his teaching on the greatest of all the commandments. All his other teachings in Mark 12 are not read in Year B. Because so much of this section of the Gospel isn't read at the Sunday Eucharist, I would

like to suggest that you take some time and read Mark 11:1–12:27 for yourself. It will set the right context for you to understand today's reading more fully.

Jesus finds himself in a debate with a scribe. Previous controversies between Jesus and the Jewish scribes proved to be bitter experiences. But this one is friendly. Since the Jewish law had 613 different commandments, the scribe wants Jesus' view on which is the greatest. Jesus doesn't quite answer the scribe's question as it is put to him, but quotes from the Jewish scriptures. He identifies the "first" commandment as the one to love God (Deuteronomy 6:4b-5) and the "second" as the commandment to love the neighbour (Leviticus 19:18). When Jesus quotes Deuteronomy 6, he is referring to the great Jewish prayer known as the *Shem'a Yisra'el* or Hear O Israel (Deuteronomy 6:4b-9). It is such a fundamental prayer that Jewish people recited it daily, in the morning and in the evening. It would be worth your while looking it up in your Bible. In quoting this prayer Jesus declares that love of God is an absolute religious value because God first loved all people and the only

The Year of the Suffering Servant

response people can make to that fact is to love God. This was a fundamental value for Jewish people of the first century AD and now Jesus establishes it as a similar essential value for his disciples.

Love of the neighbour (as oneself) implies healthy self-esteem and self-valuing. By placing this commandment alongside that of loving God, Jesus makes love of the neighbour into another way in which God is loved.

Mark adds a unique detail not found in the Synoptic Gospels (Matthew 22:34-40 and Luke 10:25-28). The scribe reacts positively to Jesus' answer, welcomes it and adds that both these commandments are "much more important than all whole burnt offerings and sacrifices." In saying this, the scribe recognizes that Jesus now replaces the entire Jewish law, along with the Temple and its rituals. This is what Jesus himself had proclaimed in his cleansing of the Temple the previous day (Mark 11:15-19). It is because the scribe is able to recognize what Jesus is doing that Jesus declares him to be "not far from the Kingdom of God."

Jesus is making an important point. Jewish people are not excluded from the Kingdom of God. Along with the Gentiles, they too are called to hear the Word of God and accept it. However, Mark doesn't tell us whether the scribe became a disciple or not. At the end of the encounter Jesus' authority is no longer challenged by his critics. Some of them (chief priests and scribes) will return later in an effort to do away with him, but they will be defeated by his resurrection.

Coming back for another look

Read the Gospel again later in the week and think about the following:

•   It is my opinion that the Catholic Church is in retreat from the vision of Vatican II and its openness to the world and to other Christians, and is slowly seeing itself as a besieged fortress in a hostile environment. What do you think?

This reading cautions against developing an "us" versus "them" mentality, especially in relation to other Christian Churches. Jesus and the scribe do not let this happen. In their mutual affirmation of love of God and of neighbour they recognize God at work in each other. This is a text all Christians can learn from.

Thirty Second Sunday in Ordinary Time

11th November 2012

last teaching before he leaves the Temple for good. The teaching falls into two parts, both based around the key word "widow."

The first part (Mark 12:38-40) deals with the bad behaviour of the scribes. You will recall that they were the theologians or scripture scholars of the day. They interpreted the Jewish law for all others and this gave them positions of power and influence over others. Jesus' criticism is that their intellectual skill is not being used for the glory of God. On the contrary, they use it to draw attention to themselves and to seek honour. They continue to wear their long and elaborate robes in public, long after they have fulfilled their duties. They do so to be greeted with respect in the marketplace. They want special places set aside for them in synagogues and banquets. Most devastatingly, Jesus says that they make a pretence of long-winded prayers while devouring the property of widows, who were considered the most vulnerable in Jewish society. For Jesus they are simply religious hypocrites and will receive a greater condemnation for their behaviour.

The second part of Jesus' teaching (Mark 12:41-44) is prompted by the action of a poor widow. There

Preparing for Sunday
Read the Gospel: Mark 12:38-44

The explanation

It is Tuesday of the last week of Jesus' life. He has been in the holy city of Jerusalem since the previous Sunday. On this Tuesday he spends the day teaching in the Temple. Today's text tells of his

The Year of the Suffering Servant

were thirteen trumpet-shaped containers around the walls of the Court of the Women where people would throw in their contributions. Jesus is sitting at a point where he can see the people making their contributions. The rich make substantial donations, while a widow throws in two copper coins. They were the smallest coins in circulation, a bit like the one cent coins today. Financially they are almost worthless, but they represent everything the widow owns. While the rich seem to make big donations, they do so out of their wealthy surplus. On the other hand, the widow donates everything she has to live on. The contrast between her and the rich is striking.

However, the contrast between her and the scribes mentioned earlier by Jesus is even more striking. Unlike the scribes, the widow demonstrates an attitude of total surrender and trust in God. Jesus has been trying to teach this attitude to his disciples, but with limited success. Very soon he will find himself in Gethsemane where he will pray, "Abba, Father ... not what I want, but what you want." Then at Golgotha his last act will be to surrender his life in trust to God. The widow will not be in Gethsemane or at Golgotha. But if she were, she would understand perfectly.

Coming back for another look

Read the Gospel again later in the week and think about the following:

•   This is a text that needs careful reading by all in the Church, but especially by those in positions of leadership and influence. The kind of religious hypocrisy that Jesus condemns in the scribes can occur in any religion at any time. I offered my view last week that the Catholic Church is in retreat from the vision and renewal of Vatican II. For me, another sign of this is that in recent times some cardinals and bishops have begun to wear once more a long robe called the *cappa magna* which has not been used since 1969. It's a seven-metre long silken train with a huge hood lined with ermine in winter and silk in summer. Cardinals wear a red *cappa magna* while bishops wear a purple one. I do not suggest for one moment that those who wear this ridiculous garment are in any way comparable to the scribes of Jesus' day. But what does it mean that some of our Church leaders do so in Jesus' name in the midst of the worst economic recession the world has ever faced and in the context of the gravest crisis our Church has known? What does it mean in the context of Jesus' words in today's reading?

•   Jesus called his disciples to let go of so much for the sake of the Gospel – trades, possessions and families. He challenged them to give their very selves for the Gospel. Above all, they were to serve others even to the point of giving their lives as he would at Golgotha. In this regard, the widow in the Temple models Jesus' idea of discipleship for all who would follow him.

Thirty Third Sunday in Ordinary Time

18th November 2012

Preparing for Sunday

Read the Gospel: Mark 13:24-32

The explanation

Today's reading comes from Mark 13, from which we read nearly a year ago on the First Sunday of Advent (pages 10-11 above). It is still Tuesday of the last week of Jesus' life. He has just left the Temple for the last time and is now within 72 hours of his death. Having left the Temple he sits down on the Mount of Olives with his disciples who are enjoying the view of the Temple and its complex of buildings. You will recall that as they look at the city, Jesus offers a long and difficult speech which runs the length of the entire chapter (Mark 13:1-37). The text is largely a farewell speech in which he offers his final words to his disciples and encourages them regarding the crises they are going to face in the future.

The language used by Mark in this chapter is often called "apocalyptic." The term comes from the Greek word *apokálypsis* which simply means "revelation." Apocalyptic writing usually deals with visions of the end times. Very often the images used in apocalyptic writing are somewhat surreal with the intention of creating a sense of wonder at the new order that is coming about.

Jesus talks about a time in the future following a period of suffering when a series of terrifying phenomena will occur. These events will signal the end of the world as people have understood it. They will also signal the return of the Son of Man in glory and the final establishment of the Kingdom of God. Jesus is clearly talking about himself and his glorious return as Messiah to complete all that he began in his ministry and to bring to an end all opposition to God's Kingdom.

In the course of his ministry Jesus attempted to show what kind of Messiah he was called to be. His miracles and teachings all pointed to it. When people got ahead of themselves and tried to identify him with the conventional Messiah of Jewish expectation, he would have none of it. Now as he faces death and trusts that God will vindicate him, he offers the disciples a description of the Messiah he really is, using apocalyptic language from the Old Testament (Daniel 7:13). When he returns in glory as Messiah, he will send out "angels"

The Year of the Suffering Servant

will take place in their own lifetime. These particular verses (Mark 13:30-31) are difficult to interpret since the end times did not come about in his disciples' lifetime. Jesus' statement needs to be understood as apocalyptic language. By it Jesus is saying that the end is very near. Like him, the disciples must surrender their fate completely to God. The "when" and "how" ought not to matter. In fact, only the Father knows when the final triumph of the Kingdom will be.

(or messengers) who will "gather the elect" from the ends of the earth. The elect are those who have responded to the Good News with repentance and faith.

At the beginning of the chapter (Mark 13:4a), the disciples asked when these events would take place. Jesus did not quite answer their question at first, but takes it up now in the image of the fig tree. Unlike most of the trees in Israel which are evergreen, the fig tree is not. It loses its leaves in autumn and only puts out new ones in late spring. When people see the new leaves they know that summer is not far off. In the same way, when people witness the events that he speaks of, then they will know that Jesus is returning as Messiah.

Jesus then assures his disciples that these events

Coming back for another look

Read the Gospel again later in the week and think about the following:

• The language in Mark 13 is apocalyptic and as such it is not intended to be read literally. It is attempting to offer a vision of the final establishment of God's Kingdom on earth. In trying to do so, it uses highly symbolical and mythical language. Jesus is Risen Lord and sits at the right hand of God. As Risen Lord he is bringing to fulfilment that which he began in his ministry in Galilee.

Even if you and I have to pay a heavy cost for being disciples today and even if evil seems to be powerfully seductive in our world, this text declares that Jesus is victorious and soon his victory will be complete throughout the entire universe. Forever.

Solemnity of Our Lord Jesus Christ-King of the Universe

20 November 2011

Preparing for Sunday
Read the Gospel: John 18:33-37

The explanation

Pope Pius XI created this feast in 1925. The Blackshirts under Mussolini were already in power in Italy. A comical-looking rabble-rouser called Adolf Hitler had just become leader of the Nazi party in Germany. The world lay in the Great Depression and atheism was on the increase. What Pius XI was doing in creating this feast was to say to the world that despite dictatorships and economic collapse and false values, Jesus Christ was still King of the Universe.

In 1969 Pope Paul VI gave the feast its current date on the last Sunday in the liturgical year. He also established the celebration as a solemnity (which is of highest liturgical rank) and gave it a new title – *The Solemnity of Our Lord Jesus Christ King of the Universe.* The liturgical colour for the solemnity is white or gold.

Today's text comes from the Fourth Gospel's Passion Narrative (John 18:1–19:42). It would be worth your while looking up John 18:1–32 in your Bible to read the text for yourself in order to understand the context for today's reading. Jesus has been arrested on the Mount of Olives and brought before Annas, the former high priest (6–15 AD). Annas questions him about his disciples and teaching and then sends him bound to Caiaphas, the current high priest (18–36 AD). These religious authorities have no power to put Jesus to death, so they then send him to Pontius Pilate who is the Governor of Judaea (26–36 AD). When Pilate realizes that they want Jesus to be executed he goes and interrogates him. This is where our text picks up the story.

Pilate questions Jesus about being a "king." This is found also in the other Gospels (Matthew 27:11; Mark 15:2 and Luke 23:3). However, the writer of the Fourth Gospel makes this the central accusation against Jesus in the Roman trial. The term "king" as used in this scene has both a political and theological meaning and the Gospel plays both these meanings off each other. For Pilate, Jesus the "King of the Jews" is someone who poses a threat to Roman rule in Judaea. For the writer of the Gospel, the title is all about Jesus' identity as Messiah and incarnate Word of God. Notice that even though Pilate is in charge of the trial, it is Jesus who becomes the interrogator! "Am I a Jew?" Pilate asks. Notice the tone of the question. He has utter contempt for the Jews and everything to do with them. There is wonderful irony here. You will recall the evangelist uses the phrase "the Jews" to describe those Jewish people who resist Jesus' message. While Pilate contemptuously rejects the idea that he is a Jew, his rejection of Jesus will put him among "the Jews."

Jesus now describes what his own kingdom is not. His kingdom "is not from this world." It "is not from here." Jesus comes from God and that is where his kingdom has its origins. If his kingdom were a mere earthly one, his "followers" would fight on his behalf. Again there is wonderful irony in the text. In talking about Jesus' "followers" the Greek text uses the same word to describe the Jewish Temple police. Jesus' kingdom does not have to be secured by force, unlike Roman rule under Pilate. He still thinks that Jesus must be a political king for he asks, "So you are a king?" Jesus' answer recalls the language of John 10 and his discourse on the Good Shepherd which we read on the Fourth Sunday of Easter (pages 76-77 above). Every disciple who recognizes the fullness of God revealed in Jesus "belongs to the truth" and hears God's words in Jesus' voice. This is what it means to accept Jesus as "king."

Coming back for another look

Read the Gospel again later in the week and think about the following:

- We humans are complex creatures. In our weakness, we can be possessed by evil. In our fragility, we can be closed down by pain. Yet in our endurance, we can be stretched by love. We live in extremely difficult times. Our Church is in a right mess, largely of the institution's own making. Yet today we remember that Pius XI created this feast to help us face the harsh realities of life. The message of this feast is that we have a hope-filled future and that things will get better for our Church if we can only open ourselves to the teaching, life and rule of our Universal King, Jesus the Christ, God's Suffering Servant.

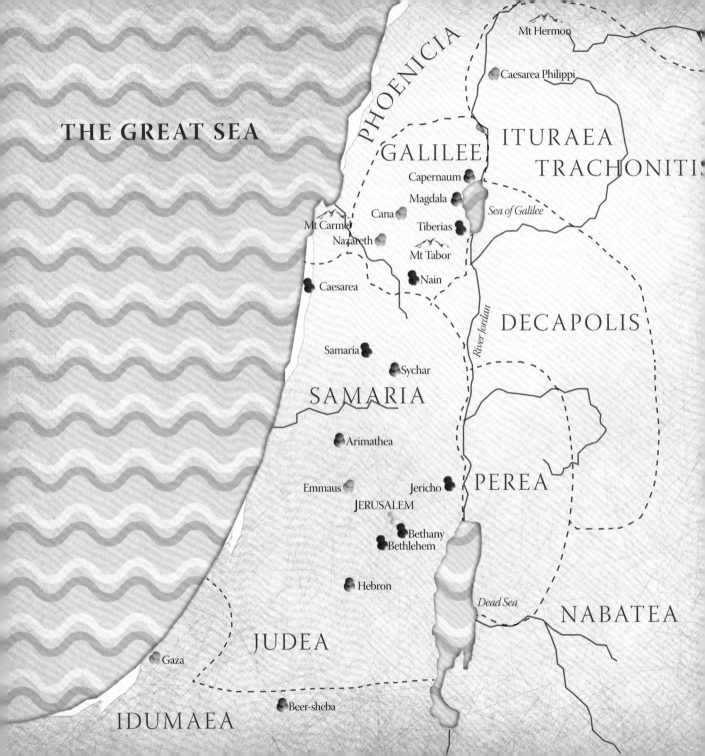